Certificate in Business Accounting

Paper C2

Financial Accounting Fundamentals

ASSESSMENT KIT

CIMA

FTC Foulks Lynch
A **Kaplan Professional** Company

British Library Cataloguing-in-Publication Data

A catalogue record for this book is available from the British Library.

Published by FTC Foulks Lynch
Swift House
Market Place
Wokingham
Berkshire
RG40 1AP

ISBN 1 84390 461 6

© The Financial Training Company Ltd, 2004

Printed and bound in Great Britain

Acknowledgements

We are grateful to the Chartered Institute of Management Accountants, the Association of Chartered Certified Accountants and the Institute of Chartered Accountants in England and Wales for permission to reproduce past examination questions. The answers have been prepared by FTC Foulks Lynch.

INTRODUCTION

We have worked closely with experienced CIMA tutors and lecturers to ensure that our Kits are assessment-focused and user-friendly.

This Assessment Kit includes an extensive selection of questions that entirely cover the syllabus – this ensures that your knowledge is tested across all syllabus areas. All questions in the Kit are grouped by syllabus topics with separate sections for 'objective test questions' and 'practice questions'

All questions are of assessment standard and format – this enables you to master the assessment techniques.

There is a mock at the back of the book – try it under timed conditions and this will give you an exact idea of the way you will be tested in your assessment.

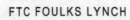

CONTENTS

INDEX TO QUESTIONS AND ANSWERS

Financial statements and ratio analysis

SYLLABUS AND LEARNING OUTCOMES

Syllabus overview

This is an introduction to financial accounting and assumes no prior knowledge of the subject. It deals with the recording of accounting transactions and the preparation of accounting statements for single entities. The basic concepts of accounting are dealt with, and the student will be expected to understand the limitations of financial accounts in attempting to meet the needs of all users. An understanding of the different approaches to asset valuation and the resulting influence on profit measurement is required.

There is an introduction to the regulatory framework that determines published accounts requirements and a basic introduction to the role of accounting standards. An awareness of published accounts is required, but students will not be asked to prepare accounts in a published accounting format. No knowledge of any specific accounting standard is required. There will be an introduction to accounting systems and their control.

Although the emphasis is on the basic methods and techniques of the subject, students will be expected to develop a critical approach by asking why the methods and techniques are used and in what circumstances they are appropriate.

This syllabus addresses the fundamentals of the subject and recognises that some terms and definitions vary from one area of the world to another. As a result, students can use accepted alternative names to those that appear in this syllabus and be aware of alternative accounting formats. For example, International Accounting Standard 1 (IAS 1) uses *income statement* instead of profit and loss account and n*on-current assets* instead of fixed assets. Others include i*nventories, receivables* and *payables*. All of these are acceptable for use in answers in this paper, but it will be expected that they are applied consistently. Similarly, IAS 1 provides illustrations of accounting formats that are used widely in published accounts and are acceptable in this paper.

Aim

This syllabus aims to test the student's ability to:

- explain the conceptual and regulatory framework of accounting;

- explain the nature of accounting systems and understand the control of such systems;

- prepare accounts for a single entity.

Learning outcomes and syllabus content

(i) CONCEPTUAL AND REGULATORY FRAMEWORK – 20%

Learning outcomes

On completion of their studies students should be able to:

- identify the various user groups which need accounting information and the characteristics of such information necessary to meet their objectives;
- explain the function of and differences between financial and management accounting systems;
- identify and explain the fundamental accounting concepts, bases and policies;
- explain the concepts of capital and revenue, cash and profit, income and expenditure and assets and liabilities;
- explain the historical cost convention;
- identify the basic methods of valuing assets on current cost, market value and economic value bases, and demonstrate their impact on profit measures and balance sheet values;
- explain the influence of legislation (for example, Companies Acts) and accounting standards on the production of published accounting information for organisations.

Syllabus content

- Users of accounts and the objectives of financial statements; functions of financial and management accounts; purpose of accounting statements; stewardship; the accounting equation.
- Fundamental accounting concepts, bases and policies; capital and revenue; cash and profit; income, expenditure, assets and liabilities.
- Historical cost convention.
- Methods of asset valuation and their implications for profit measurement and the balance sheet.
- The regulatory influence of company law and accounting standards; items in formats for published accounts.

(ii) ACCOUNTING SYSTEMS – 20%

Learning outcomes

On completion of their studies students should be able to:

- explain the purpose of accounting records and their role in the accounting system;
- prepare cash and bank accounts; prepare bank reconciliation statements;
- prepare petty cash statements under an imprest system;
- prepare accounts for sales and purchases, including personal accounts and control accounts;
- identify the necessity for financial accounting codes and construct a simple coding system;
- prepare nominal ledger accounts; prepare journal entries; prepare a trial balance;
- prepare accounts for indirect taxes (for example, VAT);
- prepare accounts for payroll.

Syllabus content

- The accounting system and accounting records.
- Ledger accounts; double-entry bookkeeping.
- Preparation of accounts for cash and bank; bank reconciliations; imprest system for petty cash.

- Accounting for sales and purchases, including personal accounts and control accounts.
- Financial accounting codes and their uses.
- Nominal ledger accounting; journal entries.
- Trial balance.
- Accounting for indirect taxes (for example, VAT).
- Accounting for payroll.

(iii) CONTROL OF ACCOUNTING SYSTEMS – 15%

Learning outcomes

- The accounting system and accounting records.
- Ledger accounts; double-entry bookkeeping.
- Preparation of accounts for cash and bank; bank reconciliations; imprest system for petty cash.
- Accounting for sales and purchases, including personal accounts and control accounts.
- Financial accounting codes and their uses.
- Nominal ledger accounting; journal entries.
- Trial balance.
- Accounting for indirect taxes (for example, VAT).
- Accounting for payroll

Syllabus content

- The purpose of external audit and the meaning of true and fair view
- Internal audit
- Financial controls; audit checks on financial controls; audit trails
- Errors or fraud.

(iv) PREPARATION OF ACCOUNTS – 45%

Learning outcomes

On completion of their studies students should be able to:

- prepare accounts using accruals and prepayments
- explain the difference between and prepare accounts for bad debts and provisions for doubtful debts
- explain and calculate the methods of depreciation, including straight line, reducing balance and revaluation, and prepare accounts using each method
- prepare a fixed asset register
- explain, calculate and prepare accounts for stock
- prepare trading accounts, profit and loss accounts, appropriation of profit and balance sheets from trial balance
- prepare manufacturing accounts
- prepare income and expenditure accounts
- prepare accounts from incomplete records
- calculate and explain basic ratios
- prepare cash flow statements.

Syllabus content

- Adjustments to the trial balance; accruals and prepayments
- Bad debts and provision for doubtful debts

- Accounting treatment for depreciation (straight line, reducing balance and revaluation methods)

- Fixed asset register

- Accounting for stocks (excluding long-term contract work-in-progress); methods of stock valuation (FIFO, LIFO and average cost)

- Trading, profit and loss accounts and balance sheets from trial balance; accounting for the appropriations of profit

- Manufacturing accounts

- Income and expenditure accounts

- Production of accounting statements from incomplete data

- Ratios: return on capital employed; gross and net profit margins; asset turnover; debtors collection and creditors time to pay; current and quick ratios; stock turnover; gearing

- Cash flow statements.

REVISION GUIDANCE

Planning your revision

Begin by asking yourself
two questions:

how much time do I have
available for revision?

what do I need to cover during
my revision?

Remember to take into account:
- times of the day when you
  work most effectively
- other commitments
- time definitely unavailable
  (e.g. holidays)
- relaxation time.

Remember to take into account that:
- all syllabus areas are equally
  examinable
- you need more time when
  revising areas of the syllabus you
  feel least confident about
- question practice is the best form
  of revision.

Make a timetable/plan to remind yourself how much
work you have to do and when you are free to do it.
Allow some time for slippage.

Revision techniques

- Go through your notes and textbook **highlighting the important points**

- You might want to produce your own set of **summarised notes**

- **List key words** for each topic to remind you of the essential concepts

- Practice **assessment-standard questions**, under timed conditions

- **Rework questions** that you got completely wrong the first time, but only when you think
  you know the subject better

- If you get stuck on topics, **find someone to explain** them to you (your tutor or a colleague,
  for example)

- **Read recent articles** on the CIMA website and in *Insider*

- **Read** good newspapers and professional journals.

COMPUTER BASED ASSESSMENT

Format of the assessment

40 objective test questions

Total time allowed: 90 minutes

Number of marks
100

About the assessment

- The process for entering for a Computer Based Assessment (CBA) is different from entering for a paper based exam.

- Contact CIMA or look up on the CIMA website to find out where your nearest CIMA accredited CBA centre is. Contact the centre and arrange to sit the assessment.

- With CBAs the most common type of questions is 'multiple choice', where you have to choose the correct answer from a list of possible answers, but there are a variety of other **objective question types** that can be used within the system. These include true/false questions, matching pairs of text and graphic, sequencing and ranking, labelling diagrams and single and multiple numeric entry. There are also questions that carry several marks.

- You need to be sure you **know how to answer questions** of this type before you sit the assessment. You will achieve this through practice.

- Whatever the format, these questions require that you have *learnt* definitions, *know* key words and their meanings and importance, and *understand* the names and meanings of rules, concepts and theories.

- Do not attempt a CBA until you have **completed all study material** relating to it.

- **Do not skip any of the material** in the syllabus.

- Before you start the assessment make sure you understand how to use the **software**. If in doubt, ask the assessment centre staff to explain it to you.

- With CBAs, questions are **displayed on the screen** and answers are entered using keyboard and mouse.

- **Read each question** *very* carefully.

- **Double-check your answer** before committing yourself to it.

- If you are answering a multiple-choice question, eliminate first those answers that you know are definitely wrong. Then choose the most appropriate answer from those that are left.

- Remember that **only one answer to a multiple-choice question can be right**.

- Answer *every* question – if you do not know an answer, you don't lose anything by guessing. Think carefully before you **guess**.

- **Don't panic** if you realise you've answered a question incorrectly – you can always go back and change your answer.

- At the end of the assessment, you are given a **certificate showing the result** you have achieve.

Section 1

OBJECTIVE TEST QUESTIONS

CONCEPTUAL AND REGULATORY FRAMEWORK

1   The MAIN aim of accounting is to:

    A   maintain ledger accounts for every asset and liability

    B   provide financial information to users of such information

    C   produce a trial balance

    D   record every financial transaction individually.

2   Financial accounts differ from management accounts in that they:

    A   are prepared monthly for internal control purposes.

    B   contain details of costs incurred in manufacturing.

    C   are summarised and prepared mainly for external users of accounting information.

    D   provide information to enable the trial balance to be prepared.

3   The accounting concept which dictates that fixed assets should be valued at cost less accumulated depreciation, rather than at their enforced saleable value, is the:

    A   net realisable value concept

    B   prudence concept

    C   realisation concept

    D   going concern concept.

4   Stocks should be valued at the lower of cost and net realisable value. Which ONE of the following accounting concepts governs this?

    A   Consistency concept

    B   Accruals concept

    C   Prudence concept

    D   Money measurement concept

5   The term 'capital maintenance' refers to:

    A   the cost of maintaining fixed assets in good condition

    B   the cost of replacing fixed assets

    C   the raising of new capital by the issue of shares

    D   retaining sufficient profits to ensure that closing net assets are at least equal in value to net assets at the beginning of the period.

6 **The historical cost concept:**

A   records transactions from past years

B   fails to take account of changing price levels over time

C   values assets at their cost to the business, irrespective of any depreciation or other loss in value

D   is no longer used in modern accounting systems.

7 **A true and fair view is given by the accounts when:**

A   assets are stated at their true values in the balance sheet

B   they have been audited and found to be accurate

C   they fairly reflect the financial position of an organisation, sufficient for users of the accounts to make proper judgements

D   the auditors are able to certify that they contain no errors or omissions, and that no fraud has been committed.

8 **In times of rising prices, the historical cost convention has the effect of:**

A   valuing all assets at their cost to the business

B   recording goods sold at their cost price, even if they are worth less than that cost

C   understating profits and overstating balance sheet asset values

D   overstating profits and understating balance sheet asset values.

9 **Who issues Financial Reporting Standards?**

A   The Auditing Practices Board.

B   The Stock Exchange.

C   The Accounting Standards Board.

D   The Government.

10 **When preparing financial statements in periods of inflation, directors:**

A   must reduce asset values

B   must increase asset values

C   must reduce dividends

D   need make no adjustments.

11 **The concept of capital maintenance is important for:**

A   The sources of finance.

B   The measurement of profit.

C   The relationship of debt to equity.

D   The purchase of fixed assets.

12 **The profit of a business may be calculated by using which one of the following formulae?**

A   Opening capital − drawings + capital introduced − closing capital

B   Closing capital + drawings − capital introduced − opening capital

C   Opening capital + drawings − capital introduced − closing capital

D   Closing capital − drawings + capital introduced − opening capital

13 A company includes in the valuation of its closing stock some goods that were received before the year end, but for which invoices were not received until after the year end. This is in accordance with:

A   the historical cost convention

B   the accruals concept

C   the consistency concept

D   the materiality concept.

14 Why should financial statements be prepared on a consistent basis?

A   To make it easier to compare results from one year to the next.

B   To ensure that the capital of the business is maintained.

C   To ensure that no material error occurs in the financial statements.

D   To make the financial statements easier to understand.

15 In times of falling prices, the historical cost convention:

A   understates asset values and profits

B   understates asset values and overstates profits

C   overstates asset values and profits

D   overstates asset values and understates profits.

16 Which one of the following sentences does NOT explain the distinction between financial accounts and management accounts?

A   Financial accounts are primarily for external users and management accounts are primarily for internal users.

B   Financial accounts are normally produced annually and management accounts are normally produced monthly.

C   Financial accounts are more accurate than management accounts.

D   Financial accounts are audited by an external auditor and management accounts do not normally have an external audit.

17 Who has the responsibility for ensuring that a company maintains proper accounting records?

A   The shareholders

B   The auditors

C   The directors

D   The company secretary

18 Which of the following best explains what is meant by 'capital expenditure'?

Capital expenditure is expenditure:

A   on fixed assets, including repairs and maintenance

B   on expensive assets

C   relating to the issue of share capital

D   relating to the acquisition or improvement of fixed assets.

19 Ensuring that the assets of a company are properly safeguarded and utilised efficiently and effectively is part of:

    A   the stewardship function exercised by the directors

    B   the external auditor's responsibility

    C   the function of the financial accountant

    D   the internal auditor's responsibility.

20 Which one of the following should be accounted for as capital expenditure?

    A   The cost of painting a building.

    B   The replacement of windows in a building.

    C   The purchase of a car by a garage for re-sale.

    D   Legal fees incurred on the purchase of a building.

21 The accounting equation can be rewritten as:

    A   assets plus profit less drawings less liabilities equals closing capital

    B   assets less liabilities less drawings equals opening capital plus profit

    C   assets less liabilities less opening capital plus drawings equals profit

    D   opening capital plus profit less drawings less liabilities equals assets.

22 A business commenced with capital in cash of £1,000. Stock costing £800 is purchased on credit, and half is sold for £1,000 plus VAT at 17.5%, the customer paying in cash at once.

The accounting equation after these transactions would show:

    A   Assets £1,775 less Liabilities £175 equals Capital £1,600

    B   Assets £2,175 less Liabilities £975 equals Capital £1,200

    C   Assets £2,575 less Liabilities £800 equals Capital £1,775

    D   Assets £2,575 less Liabilities £975 equals Capital £1,600

23 A sole trader had opening capital of £10,000 and closing capital of £4,500. During the period, the owner introduced capital of £4,000 and withdrew £8,000 for her own use.

Her profit or loss during the period was:

    A   £9,500 loss

    B   £1,500 loss

    C   £7,500 profit

    D   £17,500 profit.

24 Which ONE of the following best describes the stewardship function?

    A   Ensuring high profits.

    B   Managing cash.

    C   Ensuring the recording, controlling and safeguarding of assets.

    D   Ensuring high dividends to shareholders.

ACCOUNTING SYSTEMS

25   A sales ledger control account had a closing balance of £8,500. It contained a contra to the purchase ledger of £400, but this had been entered on the wrong side of the sales ledger control account.

The correct balance on the control account should be:

£

Data for questions 26 and 27

The cash book of Lofty Ladders shows an overdraft balance of £4,360 as at 31st December 20X3. On comparing a bank statement with the cash book, it is found that the following items have not been recorded in the cash book.

1   Bank charges of £120 and bank overdraft interest of £90

2   A credit transfer from a customer of £2,500

3   A direct debit payment to a supplier of £1,700.

It is also noticed that the following items have been recorded in the cash book but do not appear in the bank statement.

1   Cheques received from customers £3,600

2   Cheques drawn in favour of suppliers £4,200

---

26   **What figure will be shown in the balance sheet as at 31st December 20X3 for 'bank overdraft'?**

£

27   **What figure will be shown in the bank statement for the overdraft balance?**

£

28   **Which ONE of the following is a book of prime entry AND part of the double-entry system?**

A   The journal
B   The petty cash book
C   The sales day book
D   The purchase ledger

29   **You are provided with the following information relating to a business:**

	£000
Creditors' opening balance	540
Cash paid to creditors	1,470
Cash purchases	57
Credit purchases	1,590
Credit notes received from creditors	33
Discounts received from creditors	24

The Creditors' closing balance is:

£

30 **A summary of the transactions of Ramsgate, who is registered for VAT at 17.5%, shows the following for the month of August 20X9.**

Outputs   £60,000 (exclusive of VAT)

Inputs   £40,286 (inclusive of VAT)

At the beginning of the period Ramsgate owed £3,400 to Customs & Excise, and during the period he has paid £2,600 to them.

At the end of the period the amount owing to Customs & Excise is:

A   £3,700

B   £3,930

C   £4,400

D   £5,300.

31 **A trader who is not registered for VAT purposes buys goods on credit. These goods have a list price of £2,000 and the trader is given a trade discount of 20%. The goods carry VAT at 17.5%.**

The correct ledger entries to record this purchase are to debit the Purchases account and to credit the Supplier's account with:

A   £1,600

B   £1,880

C   £2,000

D   £2,350.

32 **The purchase day book of Arbroath has been undercast by £500, and the sales day book has been overcast by £700. Arbroath maintains purchase and sales ledger control accounts as part of the double entry bookkeeping system.**

The effect of correcting these errors will be to:

A   make adjustments to the ledger balances of the individual debtors and creditors, with no effect on profit

B   make adjustments to the ledger balances of the individual debtors and creditors, with a decrease in profit of £1,200

C   make adjustments to the control accounts, with no effect on profit

D   make adjustments to the control accounts, with a decrease in profit of £1,200.

33 **Stranraer Ltd provides you with the following details relating to wages paid:**

Gross wages   £157,326

Employer's NI   £33,247

PAYE and NI deducted   £44,174

At the beginning of the year Stranraer Ltd owed £7,308 to the Inland Revenue.

The total charge for wages for the year will be:

A   £183,265

B   £190,573

C   £197,881

D   £234,747.

34 You are given the following figures relating to a business's purchases and trade creditors:

	£
Creditors at 1 November 20X6	76,104
Creditors at 31 October 20X7	80,643
Purchases	286,932
Cash paid to suppliers	271,845
Discounts received	5,698
Debit balances transferred to debtors' ledger	107
Credit balances offset against debtors' ledger debit balances	866
Sundry minor credit balances written off	82

The amount of purchases returned to suppliers during the year ending 31 October 20X7 was:

£

35 For the month of November 20X0 Figgins Ltd's purchases totalled £225,600 with VAT of £33,840. The total of £259,440 has been credited to the creditors' ledger control account as £254,940.

Which of the following adjustments is correct?

	Control account	*List of creditors' balances*
A	£4,500 Cr	No adjustment
B	£4,500 Cr	Increase by £4,500
C	£29,340 Dr	No effect
D	£33,840 Dr	Increase by £4,500

36 A supplier sends you a statement showing a balance outstanding of £14,350. Your own records show a balance outstanding of £14,500.

The reason for this difference could be that:

A the supplier sent an invoice for £150 which you have not yet received

B the supplier has allowed you £150 cash discount which you had omitted to enter in your ledgers

C you have paid the supplier £150 which he has not yet accounted for

D you have returned goods worth £150 which the supplier has not yet accounted for.

37 The sales account is:

A credited with the total of sales made, including VAT

B credited with the total of sales made, excluding VAT

C debited with the total of sales made, including VAT

D debited with the total of sales made, excluding VAT.

38 Which of the following items appear on the same side of the trial balance?

A Drawings and accruals

B Carriage outwards and prepayments

C Carriage inwards and rental income

D Opening stock and purchase returns

39 A credit balance on a ledger account indicates:

A   an asset or an expense

B   a liability or an expense

C   an amount owing to the organisation

D   a liability or a revenue.

40 Andrea started a taxi business by transferring her car, worth £5,000, into the business. What are the accounting entries required to record this?

A   Dr Capital £5,000, Cr Car £5,000

B   Dr Car £5,000, Cr Drawings £5,000

C   Dr Car £5,000, Cr Capital £5,000

D   Dr Car £5,000, Credit Bank £5,000

41 A business sold goods that had a net value of £600 to Lucid plc. What entries are required to record this transaction if VAT is payable at 17.5%?

A   Dr Lucid plc £600, Dr VAT £105, Cr Sales £705

B   Dr Lucid plc £705, Cr VAT £105, Cr Sales £600

C   Dr Lucid plc £600, Cr VAT £105, Cr Sales £600

D   Dr Sales £600, Dr VAT £105, Cr Lucid plc £705

42 Laker Ltd returned goods that had a net value of £200. What entries are required to record this transaction if VAT is payable at 17.5%?

A   Dr Returns inward £200, Dr VAT £35, Cr Laker Ltd £235

B   Dr Returns inward £235, Cr VAT £35, Cr Laker Ltd £200

C   Dr Purchases £200, Dr VAT £35, Cr Laker Ltd £235

D   Dr Laker Ltd £235, Cr Returns inward £200, Cr VAT £35

43 Which of the following best describes the entries that are made using the sales day book totals at the end of each month?

A   Debit sales with total net sales, credit sales ledger control with total gross sales and credit VAT with total VAT

B   Debit sales with total gross sales, credit sales ledger control with total net sales and credit VAT with total VAT

C   Debit sales ledger control with total net sales, debit VAT with total VAT and credit sales with total gross sales

D   Debit sales ledger control with total gross sales, credit sales with total net sales and credit VAT with total VAT

44 Which of the following would NOT lead to a difference between the total of the balances on the sales ledger and the balance on the sales ledger control account?

A   An error in totalling the sales day book

B   An error in totalling the receipts column of the cash book

C   An overstatement of an entry in a debtor's account

D   An entry posted to the wrong debtor's account

45 Anthony receives goods from Brad on credit terms and Anthony subsequently pays by cheque. Anthony then discovers that the goods are faulty and cancels the cheque before it is cashed by Brad.

How should Anthony record the cancellation of the cheque in his books?

A   Debit creditors   Credit returns outwards

B   Credit bank   Debit creditors

C   Debit bank   Credit creditors

D   Credit creditors   Debit returns outwards

46 A bank statement for Gorgon Trading shows a balance of £825 overdrawn. The bank statement includes bank charges of £50, which have not been entered in the cash book.

There are unpresented cheques totalling £475 and deposits not yet credited of £800. The bank statement incorrectly shows a direct debit payment of £160, which belongs to another customer.

The figure for the bank balance in the balance sheet should be overdrawn by:

£ _____

47 Which ONE of the following might explain a debit balance on a purchase ledger account?

A   The company took a cash discount to which it was not entitled and paid less than the amount due.

B   The company mistakenly paid too much.

C   The book-keeper failed to enter a contra with the sales ledger.

D   The book-keeper failed to post a cheque paid to the account.

48 The following information relates to a bank reconciliation.

1   The bank balance in the cash book before taking the items below into account was £8,970 overdrawn.

2   Bank charges of £550 on the bank statement have not been entered in the cashbook.

3   The bank has credited the account in error with £425 which belongs to another customer.

4   Cheque payments totalling £3,275 have been entered in the cashbook but have not been presented for payment.

5   Cheques totalling £5,380 have been correctly entered on the debit side of the cashbook but have not been paid in at the bank.

What was the balance as shown by the bank statement before taking the items above into account?

A   £8,970 overdrawn.

B   £11,200 overdrawn.

C   £12,050 overdrawn.

D   £17,750 overdrawn.

49 A business had a balance at the bank of £2,500 at the start of the month. During the following month, it paid for materials invoiced at £1,000 less trade discount of 20% and cash discount of 10% of the invoice amount.

It received a cheque from a debtor in respect of an invoice for £200, subject to cash discount of 5%.

The balance at the bank at the end of the month was:

£ _____

50 **Your purchase ledger control account has a balance at 1 October 20X8 of £34,500 credit.**

During October, credit purchases were £78,400, cash purchases were £2,400 and payments made to suppliers, excluding cash purchases, and after deducting cash discounts of £1,200, were £68,900. Purchase returns were £4,700.

The closing balance was:

A   £38,100

B   £40,500

C   £47,500

D   £49,900.

51 **Your firm's bank statement at 31 October 20X8 shows a balance of £13,400. You subsequently discover that the bank has dishonoured a customer's cheque for £300 and has charged bank charges of £50, neither of which is recorded in your cash book.**

There are unpresented cheques totalling £1,400. You further discover that an automatic receipt from a customer of £195 has been recorded as a credit in your cash book.

Your cash book balance, prior to correcting the errors and omissions, was:

A   £11,455

B   £11,960

C   £12,000

D   £12,155.

52 **The petty cash imprest is restored to £100 at the end of each week. The following amounts are paid out of petty cash during week 23:**

Stationery including VAT at 17.5%	£14.10
Travelling costs	£25.50
Office refreshments	£12.90
Sundry creditors	£24.00 plus VAT at 17.5%

The amount required to restore the imprest to £100 is:

A   £19.30

B   £25.60

C   £74.40

D   £80.70.

53 **It is important to produce a trial balance prior to preparing the final accounts because:**

A   it confirms the accuracy of the ledger accounts

B   it provides all the figures necessary to prepare the final accounts

C   it shows that the ledger accounts contain debit and credit entries of an equal value

D   it enables the accountant to calculate any adjustments required.

54 **The following sales ledger control account contains some inaccurate entries.**

Sales ledger control account

	£		£
Opening debtors	14,500	Credit sales	53,500
Discounts allowed	350	Returns	1,400
Receipts from debtors	51,200	Contra to purchase ledger	50

The correct closing debtors figure should be:

£ [   ]

55 **A sales ledger control account showed a debit balance of £37,642. The individual debtors' accounts in the sales ledger showed a total of £35,840. The difference could be due to:**

A   undercasting the sales day book by £1,802

B   overcasting the sales returns day book by £1,802

C   entering a cash receipt of £1,802 on the debit side of a debtor's account

D   entering cash discount allowed of £901 on the debit side of the control account.

56 **Which of the following are used in a coding system for accounting transactions?**

A   Department code

B   Nominal ledger code

C   Product code

D   All of the above

57 **The entries in a sales ledger control account are:**

Sales	£250,000
Bank	£225,000
Returns	£2,500
Bad debts	£3,000
Returned unpaid cheque	£3,500
Contra purchase ledger account	£4,000

What is the balance on the sales ledger control account?

A   £12,000

B   £19,000

C   £25,000

D   £27,000

58 **An imprest system is:**

A   accounting computer software

B   an audit process

C   automatic agreement of the cash book and bank statement

D   a method of controlling petty cash.

59 **The total cost of salaries charged to the profit and loss account is:**

A   the total gross salaries plus employer's national insurance contributions

B   the total gross salaries

C   the total net salaries

D   the total net salaries plus employer's national insurance contributions.

60 **Which ONE of the following is a record of prime entry?**

A   The nominal ledger

B   The sales ledger

C   The trial balance

D   The sales day book

61 S Ltd, which is registered for the purposes of value added tax, bought furniture on credit terms at a cost of $8,000, plus value added tax of $1,200.

What is the correct account entry?

		DR $	CR $
A	Furniture	9,200	
	Supplier		9,200
B	Furniture	8,000	
	VAT		1,200
	Supplier		6,800
C	Furniture	8,000	
	VAT	1,200	
	Supplier		9,200
D	Furniture	8,000	
	Supplier		8,000

62 S is employed by T Ltd. His pay details for January and February are as follows:

January: Gross salary $2,000, Tax $500, National Insurance $100, Net pay $1,400

February: Gross salary $2,200, Tax $560, National Insurance $100, Net pay $1,540

Tax and National Insurance are payable to the government one month after they are deducted from employees' salaries.

How much cash did T Ltd pay out in February in connection with S's wages?

A $2,000

B $2,060

C $2,140

D $2,200

63 Which ONE of the following might explain the debit balance on a purchase ledger account?

A The company took a cash discount to which it was not entitled and paid less than the amount due.

B The company mistakenly paid too much.

C The book-keeper failed to enter a contra with the sales ledger.

D The book-keeper failed to post a cheque paid to the account.

64 B is a builder with a staff of ten employees. In April 20X1, he paid the following amounts:

- net salaries after tax and national insurance £14,000

- tax and employees' national insurance for March 20X1 £5,000

- employer's national insurance for March 20X1 £1,400.

He owes the following amounts in respect of tax and national insurance for April 20X1:

- tax and employees' national insurance   £6,000

- employer's national insurance   £1,500

The correct expense for employee costs to be shown in the profit and loss account for April 20X1 is:

A £19,000

B £20,000

C £20,400

D £21,500

65 **An employee has a gross monthly salary of £1,000. In September the tax deducted was £200, the employee's national insurance was £60, and the employer's national insurance was £100. What was the charge for salaries in the profit and loss account?**

A £740

B £940

C £1,000

D £1,100

66 **W Ltd is registered for value added tax. The managing director has asked four staff in the accounts department why the output tax for the last quarter does not equal 17.5 per cent of sales (17.5 percent is the rate of value added tax). Which one of the following four replies she received was not correct?**

A The company had some exports that were not liable to VAT.

B The company made some sales of zero-rated products.

C The company made some sales of exempt products.

B The company sold some products to businesses not registered for VAT

67 **Which of the following is not the purpose of a sales ledger control account?**

A A sales ledger control account provides a check on the arithmetic accuracy of the personal ledger.

B A sales ledger control account helps to locate errors in the trial balance.

C A sales ledger control account ensures that there are no errors in the personal ledger.

D Control accounts deter fraud.

68 **The following bank reconciliation is prepared for Brechin for the month of November 20X7**

	£	£
Balance per bank statement		18,040
Add: Lodgement in transit		4,150
		22,190
Less: Outstanding cheques	6,300	
Bank credit recorded in error	20	
		(6,320)
Balance per cash book 30 November 20X7		15,870

Bank statements for December showed:

	£
Deposits	26,100
Disbursements	22,420
Balance 31 December 20X7	21,720

All items that were outstanding at 30 November were cleared in December, including the bank credit. £2,500 in cheques were outstanding at 31 December.

What is the balance per the cash book at 31 December 20X7?

A   £19,220

B   £19,240

C   £21,720

D   £24,220

69   **Wimborne's bank statement shows a balance of £715 overdrawn. The statement includes bank charges of £74 which have not been entered in the cash book. There are also unpresented cheques totalling £824 and lodgements not yet credited of £337. In addition the bank statement erroneously includes a dividend receipt of £25 belonging to another customer.**

The bank overdraft in the balance sheet should be:

A   £253

B   £1,177

C   £1,202

D   £1,227

70   **The cash book shows a bank balance of £5,675 overdrawn at 31 August 20X5. It is subsequently discovered that a standing order for £125 has been entered twice, and that a dishonoured cheque for £450 has been debited in the cash book instead of credited.**

The correct bank balance should be:

A   £5,100 overdrawn

B   £6,000 overdrawn

C   £6,250 overdrawn

D   £6,450 overdrawn.

71   **On 1 January 20X3 Tipton Ltd's debtors were £10,000. The following relates to the year ended 31 December 20X3:**

	£
Sales	100,000
Cash receipts	90,000
Discounts allowed	800
Discounts received	700

Cash receipts include £1,000 in respect of a debtor previously written off.

On 31 December 20X3 debtors were:

A   £19,200

B   £20,200

C   £20,300

D   £20,900

72   **An organisation's cash book has an opening balance in the bank column of £485 credit. The following transactions then took place:**

Cash sales £1,450 including VAT of £150.

Receipts from customers of debts of £2,400.

Payments to creditors of debts of £1,800 less 5% cash discount.

Dishonoured cheques from customers amounting to £250.

The resulting balance in the bank column of the cash book should be:

A   £1,255 debit

B   £1,405 debit

C   £1,905 credit

D   £2,375 credit

73   **From the following information, calculate the value of purchases:**

	£
Opening creditors	142,600
Cash paid	542,300
Discounts received	13,200
Goods returned	27,500
Closing creditors	137,800

A   £302,600

B   £506,400

C   £523,200

D   £578,200

74   **You are given the following information:**

Debtors at 1 January 20X3	£10,000
Debtors at 31 December 20X3	£9,000
Total receipts during 20X3	£85,000
(including cash sales of £5,000)	

Sales on credit during 20X3 amount to:

A   £81,000

B   £86,000

C   £79,000

D   £84,000

75   **A book of prime entry is one in which:**

A   the rules of double-entry book-keeping do not apply

B   ledger accounts are maintained

C   transactions are entered prior to being recorded in the ledger accounts

D   subsidiary accounts are kept.

76   **The double-entry system of book-keeping normally results in which of the following balances on the ledger accounts?**

	Debit balances:	*Credit balances:*
A	Assets and revenues	Liabilities, capital and expenses
B	Revenues, capital and liabilities	Assets and expenses
C	Assets and expenses	Liabilities, capital and revenues
D	Assets, expenses and capital	Liabilities and revenues

77 The bank statement at 31 October 20X7 showed an overdraft of £800. On reconciling the bank statement, it was discovered that a cheque drawn by your company for £80 had not been presented for payment, and that a cheque for £130 from a customer had been dishonoured on 30 October 20X7, but that this had not yet been notified to you by the bank.

The correct bank balance to be shown in the balance sheet at 31 October 20X7 is:

A £1,010 overdrawn

B £880 overdrawn

C £750 overdrawn

D £720 overdrawn.

78 A credit entry of £450 on X's account in the books of Y could have arisen by:

A X buying goods on credit from Y

B Y paying X £450

C Y returning goods to X

D X returning goods to Y.

79 Your firm's cash book at 30 April 20X8 shows a balance at the bank of £2,490. Comparison with the bank statement at the same date reveals the following differences:

	£
Unpresented cheques	840
Bank charges not in cash book	50
Receipts not yet credited by the bank	470
Dishonoured cheque not in cash book	140

The correct bank balance at 30 April 20X8 is:

A £1,460

B £2,300

C £2,580

D £3,140

80 A sole trader's business made a profit of £32,500 during the year ended 31 March 20X8. This figure was after deducting £100 per week wages for himself. In addition, he put his home telephone bill through the business books, amounting to £400 plus VAT at 17.5%. He is registered for VAT and therefore has charged only the net amount to his profit and loss account.

His capital at 1 April 20X7 was £6,500. His capital at 31 March 20X8 was:

A £33,730

B £33,800

C £38,930

D £39,000

81   An employee is paid at the rate of £3.50 per hour. Earnings of more than £75 a week are taxed at 20%. Employees' National Insurance is 7%, and Employer's National Insurance is 10%. During week 24, the employee works for 36 hours.

The amounts to be charged to the profit and loss account and paid to the employee are:

	Profit and loss account	*Paid to employee*
A	£126.00	£94.38
B	£126.00	£106.98
C	£138.60	£94.38
D	£138.60	£106.98

82   Your firm's cash book shows a credit bank balance of £1,240 at 30 April 20X9. On comparison with the bank statement, you determine that there are unpresented cheques totalling £450, and a receipt of £140 which has not yet been passed through the bank account. The bank statement shows bank charges of £75 which have not been entered in the cash book.

The balance on the bank statement is:

A   £1,005 overdrawn

B   £930 overdrawn

C   £1,475 in credit

D   £1,550 in credit.

83   Your organisation paid £240,500 in net wages to its employees during the year. Employees' tax and national insurance amounted to £64,000 and employer's national insurance was £22,000. Employees had contributed £12,500 to a pension scheme.

The amount to be charged against profits for the year, in respect of wages is:

A   £164,000

B   £240,500

C   £262,500

D   £339,000

84   Your organisation has received a statement of account from one of its suppliers, showing an outstanding balance due to them of £1,350. On comparison with your ledger account, the following is determined:

•   Your ledger account shows a credit balance of £260.

•   The supplier has disallowed cash discount of £80 due to late payment of an invoice.

•   The supplier has not yet allowed for goods returned at the end of the period of £270.

•   Cash in transit of £830 has not been received by the supplier.

Following consideration of these items, the unreconciled difference between the two records is:

A   £70

B   £90

C   £430

D   £590

85 On 1 November 20X9, your organisation purchased, on credit from XYZ Limited, office equipment with a catalogue price of £1,000, less trade discount of 20% and cash discount of 5%, if paid for within 14 days. The correct journal entry to record the purchase on 1 November 20X9 (ignoring VAT) is:

		Debit £	Credit £
A	Office equipment	1,000	
	XYZ Limited		750
	Discount received		250
B	Office equipment	1,000	
	XYZ Limited		760
	Discount received		240
C	Office equipment	800	
	XYZ Limited		800
D	Office equipment	800	
	XYZ Limited		760
	Discount received		40

86 A business paid out £12,450 in net wages to its employees. In respect of those wages the following amounts were shown in the balance sheet:

	£
Income tax creditor	2,480
National insurance creditor – employees' contributions	1,350
National insurance creditor – employer's contributions	1,500
Pension creditor for employees' contributions	900

Employees' gross wages, before deductions, were:

A   £16,280

B   £17,180

C   £17,780

D   £18,680

87 A debit balance of £1,250 on X's account in the books of Y means that:

A   X owes £1,250 to Y

B   Y owes £1,250 to X

C   X has returned goods worth £1,250 to Y

D   X is owed £1,250 by Y.

88 In a manual accounting system, the most important reason for extracting a trial balance prior to preparing financial statements is that:

A   it proves the arithmetical accuracy of the ledgers.

B   it provides a summary of the financial statements.

C   it proves the individual ledger accounts are correct.

D   it reveals how errors have been made.

89   DEF plc has a supplier, M Ltd, and the balance on M Ltd's purchase ledger account at 31 July 20X2 was a credit balance of $2,000. On 5 August 20X2, DEF plc received the July statement from M Ltd showing a balance due of $3,000. The purchase ledger supervisor investigates the difference and discovers that:

- an invoice for $2,000 from M Ltd dated 31 July was not entered in the purchase ledger account until 3 August 20X2, but appears on M Ltd's July statement.

- a cheque for $600 sent from DEF plc to M Ltd on 25 July 20X2 in payment of a July invoice does not appear on M Ltd's July statement. This cheque was presented by M Ltd on 31 July 20X2.

The purchase ledger supervisor at DEF plc contacts the sales ledger supervisor at M Ltd and correctly says that there is a difference between the ledger accounts of:

A $400

B $1,000

C $1,400

D $1,600

90   On 1 October 20X2, the debtors' balance at G Ltd was $80,000. A summary of the transactions in the month of October is set out below.

	$
Cheques received	100,000
Contra creditors	6,000
Sales	90,000
Returns inwards	4,000
Discounts allowed	10,000

The debtors' balance at 31 October was:

A $50,000

B $58,000

C $62,000

D $70,000

91   SAD plc paid £240,000 in net wages to its employees in August 20X2. Employees' tax was £24,000, employees' national insurance was £12,000 and employer's national insurance was £14,000. Employees had contributed £6,000 to a pension scheme and had voluntarily asked for £3,000 to be deducted for charitable giving.

The amount to be charged to the profit and loss account in August 20X2 for wages is:

A   £285,000

B   £293,000

C   £296,000

D   £299,000

92   Which ONE of the following attributes is the most important for any code to possess in order to be of use in an accounting system?

A   Easy to change the code number.

B   Each code is a unique number.

C   A combination of letters and digits to ensure input accuracy.

D   Linked to assets, liabilities, income, expenditure and capital.

93 In July 20X2, a company sold goods at standard value added tax (VAT) rate with a net value of £200,000, goods exempt from VAT with a value of £50,000 and goods at zero VAT rate with a net value of £25,000. The purchases in July 20X2, which were all subject to VAT, were £161,000, including VAT. Assume that the rate of VAT is 15%.

The difference between VAT input tax and VAT output tax is:

A   Dr £9,000

B   Cr £5,850

C   Cr £9,000

D   none of these.

CONTROL OF ACCOUNTING SYSTEMS

94 An error of principle would occur if:

A   plant and machinery purchased was credited to a Fixed Assets account

B   plant and machinery purchased was debited to the Purchases account

C   plant and machinery purchased was debited to the Equipment account

D   plant and machinery purchased was debited to the correct account but with the wrong amount.

95 An error of commission is one where:

A   a transaction has not been recorded

B   one side of a transaction has been recorded in the wrong account, and that account is of a different class to the correct account

C   one side of a transaction has been recorded in the wrong account, and that account is of the same class as the correct account

D   a transaction has been recorded using the wrong amount.

96 The main purpose of an audit is to:

A   detect errors and fraud

B   ensure that the accounts are accurate

C   determine that the accounts show a true and fair view of the financial state of the organisation

D   ensure that all transactions have been recorded in the books of account.

97 A computerised spreadsheet package is most suitable for:

A   recording the dual effect of accounting transactions

B   maintaining an audit trail of transactions

C   performing bank reconciliations

D   preparing a cash budget.

98 Where a transaction is entered into the correct ledger accounts, but the wrong amount is used, the error is known as an error of:

A   omission

B   original entry

C   commission

D   principle.

99 **The responsibility for ensuring that all accounting transactions are properly recorded and summarised in the final accounts lies with:**

  A   the external auditors

  B   the internal auditors

  C   the shareholders

  D   the directors.

100 **Which ONE of the following is an error of principle?**

  A   A gas bill credited to the gas account and debited to the bank account.

  B   The purchase of a fixed asset credited to the asset at cost account and debited to the creditor's account.

  C   The purchase of a fixed asset debited to the purchases account and credited to the creditor's account.

  D   The payment of wages debited and credited to the correct accounts, but using the wrong amount.

101 **A major aim of the internal auditors is to:**

  A   reduce the costs of the external auditors by carrying out some of their duties

  B   support the work of the external auditors

  C   prepare the financial accounts

  D   report to shareholders on the accuracy of the accounts.

102 **A computerised accounts package would be MOST useful in maintaining:**

  A   the ledger accounts

  B   the books of prime entry

  C   a register of fixed assets

  D   the stock records.

103 **An error of original entry would occur if the purchase of goods for resale was:**

  A   debited and credited to the correct accounts using the incorrect amount in both cases

  B   credited to the purchases account and debited to the supplier's account

  C   debited to a fixed assets account

  D   entered correctly to the purchases account, but entered in the supplier's account using the wrong amount.

104 **Which ONE of the following is correct?**

  A   All limited companies are required by law to have an external audit.

  B   Only public limited companies are required by law to have an external audit.

  C   Only limited companies above a certain size are required by law to have an external audit.

  D   An external audit for a limited company is voluntary.

105 **The responsibility for internal control rests with:**

  A   the internal auditors.

  B   the external auditors.

  C   the shareholders.

  D   the directors.

106   A 'value for money audit' is:

    A   an external audit with limited scope

    B   a review of expenditure to ensure effectiveness, efficiency and economy

    C   a voluntary audit by an unregistered auditor

    D   none of these.

107   The segregation of duties is:

    A   delegation of duties by a manager

    B   two staff sharing one job

    C   a feature of internal control

    D   all of the above.

108   Which of the following errors will cause the trial balance totals to be unequal?

    A   Errors of transposition.

    B   Errors of omission.

    C   Errors of principle.

    D   All of the above.

109   The principal duty of an external auditor is:

    A   to check that a company's accounts agree with the accounting records

    B   to ensure that a company's systems and controls are adequate to ensure the reliability of the accounting records

    C   to prevent fraud and errors

    D   to provide a report to the shareholders.

110   Which ONE of the following provides the best definition of an 'audit trail'?

    A   The marks left by an auditor when a document has been inspected.

    B   The working papers of an auditor.

    C   The pursuit of a fraud by an auditor.

    D   The trail of a transaction from source document to financial statement.

111   The fundamental objective of an external audit of a limited company is to:

    A   give advice to shareholders

    B   detect fraud and errors

    C   measure the performance and financial position of a company

    D   provide an opinion on the financial statements.

112   Which of the following statements is correct?

    A   External auditors report to the directors.

    B   External auditors are appointed by the directors.

    C   External auditors are required to give a report to shareholders.

    D   External auditors correct errors in financial statements.

113 **Internal control includes 'detect' controls and 'prevent' controls. Which of the following is a detect control?**

A   Signing overtime claim forms.

B   Matching purchase invoices with goods received notes.

C   Preparing bank reconciliations.

D   Matching sales invoices with delivery notes.

114 **Which of the following statements is not correct?**

A   Internal auditors review value for money.

B   Internal auditors should not liaise with external auditors.

C   Internal audit is part of internal control.

D   Internal audit should be independent of the activities it audits.

115 **The trial balance of C Limited did not agree, and a suspense account was opened for the difference. Checking in the bookkeeping system revealed a number of errors:**

Error

1   £4,600 paid for motor van repairs was correctly treated in the cash book but was credited to motor vehicles asset account.

2   £360 received from Brown, a customer, was credited in error to the account of Green.

3   £9,500 paid for rent was debited to the rent account as £5,900.

4   The total of the discount allowed column in the cash book had been debited in error to the discounts received account.

5   No entries had been made to record a cash sale of £100.

Which of the errors above would require an entry to the suspense account as part of the process of correcting them?

A   Errors 3 and 4 only

B   Errors 1 and 3 only

C   Errors 2 and 5 only

D   Errors 2 and 3 only

116 **Drive Limited gives a cash discount of £40 to a customer. The discount is credited to the discounts allowed account.**

The effect of recording the discount in this way is that profit will be:

A   correct

B   overstated by £80

C   understated by £80

D   understated by £40.

117 **In reconciling the debtors' ledger control account with the list of debtor ledger balances of SK Ltd, the following errors were found:**

1   The sales day book had been overcast by £370.

2   A total of £940 from the cash receipts book had been recorded in the debtors' ledger control account as £490.

What adjustments must be made to correct the errors?

A   Credit debtors control account £820. Decrease total of sales ledger balances by £820.

B   Credit debtors control account £820. No change in total of sales ledger balances.

C   Debit debtors control account £80. No change in total of sales ledger balances.

D   Debit debtors control account £80. Increase total of sales ledger balances by £80.

118   **A suspense account was opened when a trial balance failed to agree. The following errors were later discovered:**

Error

1   A gas bill of £420 had been recorded in the Gas account as £240.

2   Discount of £50 given to a customer had been credited to Discounts Received.

3   Interest received of £70 had been entered in the bank account only.

The original balance on the suspense account was:

A   debit £210

B   credit £210

C   debit £160

D   credit £160.

119   **A trial balance has been extracted and a suspense account opened. One error relates to the misposting of an amount of £200, being discounts received from suppliers, to the wrong side of the discounts account.**

What will be the correcting journal entry?

A   Dr Discounts account £200, Cr Suspense account £200

B   Dr Suspense account £200, Cr Discounts account £200

C   Dr Discounts account £400, Cr Suspense account £400

D   Dr Suspense account £400, Cr Discounts account £400

120   **Which of the following will not cause an entry to be made in a suspense account?**

A   Drawings shown on the credit side of the trial balance

B   Discounts allowed shown on the debit side of the trial balance

C   Omission of a bad debt written off from the trial balance

D   The entry of cash in hand (£1,680) on the trial balance as £1,860

121   **On extracting a trial balance a suspense account is opened with a credit balance on it. You discover that this is caused by a single error in the nominal ledger. Which of the following could therefore have caused the imbalance?**

A   The income tax and National Insurance deductions for the current month have been entered twice in the deductions control account

B   A debtors ledger/creditors ledger contra has been entered on the credit side of both control accounts

C   The opening accrual for telephone charges has been brought forward at the beginning of the year on the wrong side of the ledger account

D   The figure of closing stock has been entered on both sides of the trial balance

122   The book-keeper of High Hurdles was instructed to make a contra entry for £270 between the supplier account and the customer for Greyfold Limited. He recorded the transaction by debiting the customer account and crediting the supplier account with £270. The business accounts do not include control accounts.

Which of the following statements is correct?

A   Unless the error is corrected, profit will be over-stated by £540.

B   Unless the error is corrected, net assets will be over-stated by £270.

C   Unless the error is corrected, net assets will be over-stated by £540.

D   The errors should be corrected, but neither the profit nor the net assets are over-stated.

123   Jones, a sole trader, has extracted a trial balance and needed to insert a suspense account to make it balance. He has discovered the following errors:

Error

1   Opening stock of £1,475 has been listed in the trial balance as a credit balance of £1,745.

2   The sales for November (£5,390 inclusive of VAT) had been correctly entered in the control account and the sales account but no entry had been made in the VAT account. The amount entered in the sales account was £4,600.

3   The opening accrual for telephone charges of £190 had been brought forward on the wrong side of the telephone expense account.

What was the suspense account balance that Jones inserted into the trial balance?

A   £2,050 Dr

B   £2,050 Cr

C   £2,840 Dr

D   £2,840 Cr

124   An accountant is attempting to resolve a suspense account difference. One of the errors relates to the misposting of an amount of £3,079 of VAT on purchases to the wrong side of the VAT account.

What will be the correcting entry?

A   Debit VAT account £6,158, Credit Suspense account £6,158

B   Debit Suspense account £6,158, Credit VAT account £6,158

C   Debit VAT account £3,079, Credit Suspense account £3,079

D   Debit Suspense account £3,079, Credit VAT account £3,079

125   Net profit was calculated as being £10,200. It was later discovered that capital expenditure of £3,000 had been treated as revenue expenditure, and revenue receipts of £1,400 had been treated as capital receipts.

The correct net profit should have been:

£ _____

126 A suspense account shows a credit balance of £130.

This could be due to:

A omitting a sale of £130 from the sales ledger

B recording a purchase of £130 twice in the purchases account

C failing to write off a bad debt of £130

D recording an electricity bill paid of £65 by debiting the bank account and crediting the electricity account.

127 Recording the purchase of computer stationery by debiting the Computer Equipment account at cost would result in:

A an overstatement of profit and an overstatement of fixed assets

B an understatement of profit and an overstatement of fixed assets

C an overstatement of profit and an understatement of fixed assets

D an understatement of profit and an understatement of fixed assets.

128 An organisation restores its petty cash balance to £500 at the end of each month. During January, the total column in the petty cash book was recorded as being £420, and hence the imprest was restored by this amount. The analysis columns, which had been posted to the nominal ledger, totalled only £400. This error would result in:

A no imbalance in the trial balance

B the trial balance being £20 higher on the debit side

C the trial balance being £20 higher on the credit side

D the petty cash balance being £20 lower than it should be.

129 A Ltd's trial balance does not balance. Which ONE of the following errors may be the cause of this failure to balance?

A The purchase of a machine had been debited to the machine repairs account.

B A cheque from a customer had been credited to the purchase ledger account of the customer.

C Goods returned inwards had been debited to the sales ledger account of the customer.

D The depreciation charge on machinery had been credited to the cost of machinery account.

130 The suspense account shows a debit balance of £100. This could be due to:

A entering £50 received from A Turner on the debit side of A Turner's account.

B entering £50 received from A Turner on the credit side of A Turner's account.

C undercasting the sales day book by £100.

D undercasting the purchases day book by £100.

131 JSL Ltd operates the imprest system for its petty cash with a float of $750. At the end of July, the cashier prepared a spreadsheet for the petty cash expenses with a total column and analysis columns. A cash voucher for petrol for $50 was incorrectly entered as $5 in the total column and also in one of the analysis columns in the spreadsheet.

The total column was posted to the cash account, the analysis columns were posted to the relevant nominal ledger accounts and cash was drawn from the bank for the total of the cash expenditure on the spreadsheet.

The effect of this error would be:

A a petty cash balance of $705.

B petrol expenses overstated by $45.

C an imbalance on the trial balance.

D a petty cash balance of $750.

132 Financial controls are primarily needed to:

A minimize the risk of fraud and error.

B comply with legal requirements.

C improve the efficiency of the business.

D reduce the expense of the external auditors.

133 The internal auditor at ILT plc has noticed that cheques from customers are being paid into the bank account approximately one month after the date on the cheque.

Should the internal auditor:

A instruct the cashier to pay cheques in more promptly?

B disregard, because all cheques have been accounted for?

C ask customers to pay more promptly?

D inform senior management there may be a fraud?

134 Which of the following functions would most benefit from segregated duties of staff?

A Separate staff to maintain the sales and purchase ledgers.

B Separate staff to maintain the personal and nominal ledger accounts.

C Separate staff to deal with the bank reconciliation and the cash book.

D Separate staff to deal with the trial balance and the preparation of accounts.

135 The trial balance of EHL plc does not balance and the debits exceed the credits by $2,300. The following errors are discovered:

- the single column manual cash book receipts column was undercast by $600
- discount received of $400 had been debited to the interest payable account
- the proceeds of $1,000 on the sale of a fixed asset had been credited to sales.

Following the correction of these errors, the balance on the suspense account would be:

A Cr $900

B Cr $2,100

C Cr $3,700

D Dr $2,100

PREPARATION OF ACCOUNTS: ACCRUALS AND PREPAYMENTS, STOCKS, DEBTORS AND FIXED ASSETS

136 A retail business has the following two items of stock at its year end.

Item	Cost	Net realisable value
	£	£
X	800	750
Y	600	640

Applying the prudence concept, what should be the valuation of this stock in the balance sheet of the business?

£

137 A business compiling its accounts for the year to 31 January each year, pays rent quarterly in advance on 1 January, 1 April, 1 July and 1 October each year. After remaining unchanged for some years, the rent was increased from £24,000 per year to £30,000 per year as from 1 July 20X3.

Which of the following figures is the rent expense which should appear in the profit and loss account for the year ended 31 January 20X4?

A   £27,500

B   £29,500

C   £28,000

D   £29,000

138 Headington is owed £37,500 by its debtors at the start, and £39,000 at the end, of its year ended 31 December 20X8.

During the period, cash sales of £263,500 and credit sales of £357,500 were made, discounts allowed amounting to £15,750 and discounts received £21,400. Bad debts of £10,500 were written off and Headington wishes to retain its provision for bad debts at 5% of total debtors.

The cash received in the year totalled:

A   £329,750

B   £593,175

C   £593,250

D   £614,650

139 How is closing stock recorded in the bookkeeping records?

A   By a debit to stock and a credit to profit and loss

B   By a debit to profit and loss and a credit to stock

C   By a debit to stock and a credit to purchases

D   By writing the figure in a note beneath the trial balance

140 A fixed asset register is:

A   an alternative name for the fixed asset ledger account

B   a list of the physical fixed assets rather than their financial cost

C   a schedule of planned maintenance of fixed assets for use by the plant engineer

D   a schedule of the cost and other information about each individual fixed asset.

141 At 30 June 20X3, an electricity ledger account had an accrual of £300 and a credit balance was brought down at 1 July 20X3. During the financial year, electricity invoices totalling £4,000 were paid, including an invoice for £600 for the quarter ended 31 May 20X4.

What is the profit and loss account charge for electricity payable for the year ended 30 June 20X4?

£ _____

142 The electricity account for the year ended 30 June 20X3 was as follows:

	£
Opening balance for electricity accrued at 1 July 20X2.	300
Payments made during the year:	
1 August 20X2 for three months to 31 July 20X2.	600
1 November 20X2 for three months to 31 October 20X2.	720
1 February 20X3 for three months to 31 January 20X3.	900
30 June 20X3 for three months to 30 April 20X3.	840

Which of the following is the appropriate entry for electricity?

	Accrued at June 20X3	Charged to profit and loss account, year ended 30 June 20X3
A	£Nil	£3,060
B	£460	£3,320
C	£560	£3,320
D	£560	£3,420

143 A company has been notified that a debtor has been declared bankrupt. The company had previously provided for this doubtful debt. Which of the following is the correct double entry?

	Debit	Credit
A	Bad and doubtful debts account	The debtor
B	The debtor	Bad and doubtful debts account
C	Provision for doubtful debts	The debtor
D	The debtor	Provision for doubtful debts

144 A business has opening stock of £12,000 and closing stock of £18,000. Purchase returns were £5,000. The cost of goods sold was £111,000.

Purchases were:

£ _____

145 After calculating your company's profit for 20X3, you discover that:

1   A fixed asset costing £50,000 has been included in the purchases account.

2   Stationery costing £10,000 has been included as closing stock of raw materials, instead of as stock of stationery.

These two errors have had the effect of:

A   understating gross profit by £40,000 and understating net profit by £50,000

B   understating both gross profit and net profit by £40,000

C   understating gross profit by £60,000 and understating net profit by £50,000

D   overstating both gross profit and net profit by £60,000.

146 Diesel fuel in stock at 1 November 20X7 was £12,500 and there were invoices awaited for £1,700. During the year to 31 October 20X8, diesel fuel bills of £85,400 were paid, and a delivery worth £1,300 had yet to be invoiced.

At 31 October 20X8, the stock of diesel fuel was valued at £9,800. The diesel fuel to be charged to the profit and loss account for the year to 31 October 20X8 is:

A   £85,100

B   £87,700

C   £88,500

D   £91,100.

147 At 31 March 20X3, accrued rent payable was £300. During the year ended 31 March 20X4, rent paid was £4,000, including an invoice for £1,200 for the quarter ended 30 April 20X4.

What is the profit and loss account charge for rent payable for the year ended 31 March 20X4?

A   £3,300

B   £3,900

C   £4,100

D   £4,700

148 The annual insurance premium for S Ltd for the period 1 July 20X3 to 30 June 20X4 is £13,200, which is 10% more than the previous year. Insurance premiums are paid on 1 July.

What is the profit and loss account charge for insurance for the year ended 31 December 20X3?

A   £11,800

B   £12,540

C   £12,600

D   £13,200

149 Vox Limited acquired a lorry on 1 May 20X4 at a cost of £60,000. It has an estimated life of four years, at the end of which it should have a resale value of £12,000.

Vox charges depreciation on a straight line basis, with a proportionate charge in the period of acquisition.

What will be the depreciation charge in the accounting period to 30 September 20X4?

£ _____

150 In times of rising prices, the FIFO method of stock valuation, when compared to the average cost method of stock valuation, will usually produce:

A   a higher profit and a lower closing stock value

B   a higher profit and a higher closing stock value

C   a lower profit and a lower closing stock value

D   a lower profit and a higher closing stock value.

151 The turnover in a company was £2 million and its debtors were 5% of turnover. The company wishes to have a provision for doubtful debts of 4% of debtors, which would make the provision one-third higher than the current provision.

How will the profit for the period be affected by the change in provision?

A   Profit will be reduced by £1,000

B   Profit will be increased by £1,000

C   Profit will be reduced by £1,333

D   Profit will be increased by £1,333

152 Brunch Ltd exchanged stock for a delivery vehicle with Trip Ltd. The stock had cost Brunch Ltd £10,000 and the normal selling price was £12,000; the delivery vehicle had cost Trip Ltd £9,000 and the normal selling price was £13,000.

How should Brunch Ltd value the vehicle in its balance sheet?

A   £9,000

B   £10,000

C   £12,000

D   £13,000

153 A car was purchased for £12,000 on 1 April 20X1 and has been depreciated at 20% each year straight line, assuming no residual value.

The company policy is to charge a full year's depreciation in the year of purchase and no depreciation in the year of sale. The car was traded in for a replacement vehicle on 1 August 20X4 for an agreed figure of £5,000.

What was the profit or loss on the disposal of the vehicle for the year ended 31 December 20X4?

A   Loss £2,200

B   Loss £1,400

C   Loss £200

D   Profit £200

154 When valuing stock at cost, which of the following shows the correct method of arriving at cost?

	Include inward transport costs	Include production overheads
A	Yes	No
B	No	Yes
C	Yes	Yes
D	No	No

155 The provision for doubtful debts in the ledger of B Ltd at 31 October 20X1 was £9,000. During the year ended 31 October 20X2, bad debts of £5,000 were written off.

Debtor balances at 31 October 20X2 were £120,000 and the company policy is to have a general provision of 5%.

What is the charge for bad and doubtful debts in the profit and loss account for the year ended 31 October 20X2?

A   £2,000

B   £3,000

C   £5,000

D   £8,000

156 A company bought a machine on 1 October 20X2 for £52,000. The machine had an expected life of eight years and an estimated residual value of £4,000.

On 31 March 20X7, the machine was sold for £35,000. The company's year end is 31 December. The company uses the straight-line method for depreciation and it charges a full year's depreciation in the year of purchase and none in the year of sale.

What is the profit or loss on disposal of the machine?

A   Loss £13,000

B   Profit £7,000

C   Profit £10,000

D   Profit £13,000

157 Nick plc purchased a machine for £15,000. The transportation costs were £1,500 and installation costs were £750.

The machine broke down at the end of the first month in use and cost £400 to repair. Nick plc depreciates machinery at 10% each year on cost, assuming no residual value.

What is the net book value of the machine after one year, to the nearest pound?

£ [   ]

158 Which one of the following lists consists only of items which may be included in the balance sheet value of a stock of finished goods manufactured by a business?

A   Foreman's wages, carriage inwards, carriage outwards, raw materials

B   Raw materials, carriage inwards, costs of storage of finished goods, plant depreciation

C   Plant depreciation, carriage inwards, raw materials, foreman's wages

D   Carriage outwards, raw materials, foreman's wages, plant depreciation

159 At 30 September 20X2, the following balances existed in the records of Lambda:

Plant and equipment:

Cost   £860,000

Accumulated depreciation   £397,000

During the year ended 30 September 20X3, plant with a written down value of £37,000 was sold for £49,000. The plant had originally cost £80,000. Plant purchased during the year cost £180,000. It is the company's policy to charge a full year's depreciation in the year of acquisition of an asset and none in the year of sale, using a rate of 10% on the straight line basis.

What net amount should appear in Lambda's balance sheet at 30 September 20X3 for plant and equipment?

A £563,000

B £467,000

C £510,000

D £606,000

160 The year-end stock of Hythe has been evaluated at £72,857. You discover that:

1 8,000 nails have been valued at £1 each, rather than £1 per hundred.

2 The running total of £6,872 on page 147 of the stock sheets has been carried forward as £8,726 on page 148.

3 200 units of component P have been included in stock at £250 each, their cost price. Their replacement cost is now £210 and the estimated net realisable value is £208, before allowing for selling expenses of £500 in total.

The correct year-end stock value should be:

£

161 Percy Pilbeam is a book wholesaler. On each sale, commission of 4% is payable to the selling agent.

The following information is available in respect of total stocks of three of his most popular titles at his financial year-end:

	Cost £	Selling price £
Henry VII – Shakespeare	2,280	2,900
Dissuasion – Jane Armstrong-Siddeley	4,080	4,000
Pilgrim's Painful Progress – John Bunion	1,280	1,300

What is the total value of these stocks in Percy's balance sheet?

A £7,368

B £7,400

C £7,560

D £7,640

162 Roberta Wickham decides to offer discounts on some of the slower-selling items in her music shop. These items are as follows at 31 March 20X0:

	Cost £	Estimated price £	Discount (% of selling price) %
Liszt – To Port	50	70	20
Delius – Myth	70	55	10
Offenbach – Up the Wrong Tree	150	225	10
Bax – To the Wall	30	35	50

What is the total stock value of the above items at 31 March 20X0?

A £267.00

B £274.00

C £300.00

D £325.50

163 **Depreciation is best described as:**

A   a means of spreading the payment for fixed assets over a period of years

B   a decline in the market value of the assets

C   a means of spreading the net cost of fixed assets over their estimated useful life

D   a means of estimating the amount of money needed to replace the assets.

164 **An organisation's fixed asset register shows a net book value of £125,600. The fixed asset account in the nominal ledger shows a net book value of £135,600.**

The difference could be due to a disposed asset not having been deducted from the fixed asset ledger:

A   with disposal proceeds of £15,000 and a profit on disposal of £5,000

B   with disposal proceeds of £15,000 and a net book value of £5,000

C   with disposal proceeds of £15,000 and a loss on disposal of £5,000

D   with disposal proceeds of £5,000 and a net book value of £5,000.

165 **At 1 July 20X8 Herne Bay Ltd has a freehold property in its books at £380,000 (cost), £278,000 (net book value). Depreciation is charged at 2% straight line.**

At the end of its accounting year ended 30 June 20X9 Herne Bay wishes to include the property at a professional valuation of £411,000, the valuation being agreed at that date.

Assuming depreciation has already been charged for the year ended 30 June 20X9, Herne Bay should:

A	Dr	Freehold property – Valuation	£411,000
	Dr	Freehold property – Accumulated depreciation	£102,000
	Cr	Freehold property – Cost	£380,000
	Cr	Revaluation reserve	£133,000
B	Dr	Freehold property – Valuation	£411,000
	Dr	Freehold property – Accumulated depreciation	£109,600
	Cr	Freehold property – Cost	£380,000
	Cr	Revaluation reserve	£140,600
C	Dr	Freehold property – Valuation	£411,000
	Dr	Freehold property – Accumulated depreciation	£278,000
	Cr	Freehold property – Cost	£380,000
	Cr	Revaluation reserve	£309,000
D	Dr	Freehold property – Valuation	£411,000
	Dr	Freehold property – Accumulated depreciation	£285,600
	Cr	Freehold property – Cost	£380,000
	Cr	Revaluation reserve	£316,600

166 **A fixed asset register showed a net book value of £67,460. A fixed asset costing £15,000 had been sold for £4,000, making a loss on disposal of £1,250.**

No entries had been made in the fixed asset register for this disposal.

After amendment, the balance on the fixed asset register will be:

£

167 **On 1 January 20X8 Wootton Ltd has a building in its books at cost £380,000, net book value £260,000.**

On 1 July 20X8 the asset is revalued at £450,000 and Wootton wishes to include that valuation in its books. Wootton's accounting policy is to depreciate buildings at 3% straight line.

The depreciation charge to profit and loss account is:

A   £8,300

B   £11,400

C   £12,450

D   £13,500.

168 **A business with a financial year-end 31 October buys a fixed asset on 1 July 20X3 for £126,000.**

Depreciation is charged at the rate of 15% per annum on the reducing balance basis. On 30 September 20X7 the asset was sold for £54,800. It is the policy of the business to charge a proportionate amount of depreciation in both the year of acquisition and the year of disposal.

What was the loss on sale of the asset (to the nearest £)?

A   £19,792

B   £8,603

C   £7,674

D   £1,106

169 **During the year ended 31 December 20X9 Follands' sales totalled £3,000,000, its debtors amounting to 4% of sales for the year.**

Follands wishes to maintain its bad debt provision at 3% of debtors, and discovers that the provision as a result is 25% higher than it was a year before.

During the year specific bad debts of £3,200 were written off and bad debts (written off three years previously) of £150 were recovered.

What is the net charge for bad and doubtful debts for the year ended 31 December 20X9?

A   £720

B   £900

C   £3,770

D   £3,950

170 **At the beginning of its accounting period a business has debtors of £13,720 after deducting a specific provision of £350 and a general provision against 2% of the remainder.**

At the year-end debtors before any provisions amount to £17,500. No specific provision is to be made but the general provision is to be increased to 3% of debtors.

What is the charge or credit in the profit and loss account in relation to bad debts for the year?

A   £525   Dr

B   £175   Dr

C   £105   Cr

D   £99   Cr

171 A bad debt written off two years ago is unexpectedly recovered and entered in the sales ledger column in the cash book.

What adjustment, if any, will be necessary – assuming that the receipt was treated as sales ledger cash?

	Debit	Credit
A	Bad debts account	Sales ledger control account
B	Sales ledger control account	Bad debts account
C	Suspense account	Bad debts account
D	No adjustment will be necessary	

172 The opening balance on Jewel plc's bad debt provision was £1,000. Jewel plc wrote off £4,000 of bad debts during the year.

The closing balance on the bad debt provision was £1,200. What is the total charge to Jewel plc's profit and loss account in respect of bad debts for the year?

£ [   ]

173 A Ltd has an item in stock which cost £1,000 and can be sold for £1,200. However, before it can be sold, it will require to be modified at a cost of £150.

The expected selling costs of the item are an additional £100.

How should this item be valued in stock?

£ [   ]

174 S & Co sell three products — Basic, Super and Luxury. The following information was available at the year end:

	Basic £ per unit	Super £ per unit	Luxury £ per unit
Original cost	6	9	18
Estimated selling price	9	12	15
Selling and distribution costs	1	4	5
	units	units	units
Units in stock	200	250	150

The value of stock at the year end should be:

A £4,200

B £4,700

C £5,700

D £6,150.

175 A car was purchased by a newsagent business in May 20X1 for:

	£
Cost	10,000
Road tax	150
Total	10,150

The business adopts a date of 31 December as its year end.

The car was traded in for a replacement vehicle in August 20X5 at an agreed value of £5,000.

It has been depreciated at 25 per cent per annum on the reducing-balance method, charging a full year's depreciation in the year of purchase and none in the year of sale.

What was the profit or loss on disposal of the vehicle during the year ended December 20X5?

A   Profit: £718

B   Profit: £781

C   Profit: £1,788

D   Profit: £1,836

176   **A stock record card shows the following details.**

February:	1	50 units in stock at a cost of £40 per unit
	7	100 units purchased at a cost of £45 per unit
	14	80 units sold
	21	50 units purchased at a cost of £50 per unit
	28	60 units sold

What is the value of stock at 28 February using the FIFO method?

£

177   **The net book value of a company's fixed assets was £200,000 at 1 August 20X2. During the year ended 31 July 20X3, the company sold fixed assets for £25,000 on which it made a loss of £5,000.**

The depreciation charge for the year was £20,000. What was the net book value of fixed assets at 31 July 20X3?

A   £150,000

B   £155,000

C   £160,000

D   £180,000

178   **Goodwill is most appropriately classed as:**

A   a current asset

B   an intangible asset

C   a fictitious liability

D   a semi-fixed asset.

179   **A fixed asset costing £12,500 was sold at a book loss of £4,500. Depreciation had been provided using the reducing balance, at 20% per annum since its purchase.**

Which of the following correctly describes the sale proceeds and length of time for which the asset had been owned?

	Sale proceeds	*Length of ownership*
A	Cannot be calculated	Cannot be calculated
B	Cannot be calculated	2 years
C	£8,000	Cannot be calculated
D	£8,000	2 years

180 Your company auditor insists that it is necessary to record items of plant separately and to depreciate them over several years, but that items of office equipment, such as hand-held stapling machines, can be grouped together and written off against profits immediately.

The main reason for this difference in treatment between the two items is because:

A   treatment of the two items must be consistent with treatment in previous periods

B   items of plant last for several years, whereas hand-held stapling machines last only for months

C   hand-held stapling machines are not regarded as material items

D   items of plant are revalued from time to time, whereas hand-held stapling machines are recorded at historical cost.

181 An increase in the provision for doubtful debts results in:

A   a decrease in current liabilities

B   an increase in net profit

C   an increase in working capital

D   a decrease in working capital.

182 The draft balance sheet of Hocket Limited at 31 December 20X4 includes the following current assets.

Stock   £87,000
Debtors   £124,000

The figure for debtors includes goods sent out on a sale or return basis at a price of £6,000 (cost £4,500). These were still unsold at 31 December 20X4.

What should be the value of stock and debtors in the balance sheet of Hocket at 31 December 20X4?

	Stock	Debtors
A	£87,000	£124,000
B	£91,500	£118,000
C	£91,500	£119,500
D	£93,000	£118,000

183 The reducing balance method of depreciating fixed assets is more appropriate than the straight-line method when:

A   there is no expected residual value for the asset

B   the expected life of the asset is not capable of being estimated

C   the asset is expected to be replaced in a short period of time

D   the asset decreases in value less in later years than in the early years of use.

184 **A company started the year with total debtors of £87,000 and a provision for doubtful debts of £2,500.**

During the year, two specific debts were written off, one for £800 and the other for £550. A debt of £350 that had been written off as bad in the previous year was paid during the year. At the year end, total debtors were £90,000 and the provision for doubtful debts was £2,300.

What is the charge to the profit and loss account for the year in respect of bad and doubtful debts?

A   £800

B   £1,000

C   £1,150

D   £1,550

185 **On 1 June, 20X0, H paid an insurance invoice of $2,400 for the year to 31 May 20X1. What is the charge to the profit and loss account and the entry in the balance sheet for the year ended 31 December 20X0?**

A $1,000 profit and loss account and prepayment of $1,400

B $1,400 profit and loss account and accrual of $1,000.

C $1,400 profit and loss account and prepayment of $1,000.

D $2,400 profit and loss account and no entry in the balance sheet.

186 **SOR Ltd's stock was valued at $13,000 and excluded goods supplied to a customer on a sale or return basis. The customer still has 30 days within which to return the stock. The goods on sale or return were purchased by SOR Ltd for $6,000 and were invoiced at a mark-up of 25%.**

The value of SOR Ltd's stock should be:

A $13,000

B $19,000

C $20,500

D $21,000

187 **S is a builder who has numerous small items of equipment. He calculates his depreciation using the revaluation method. At the beginning of his financial year he valued his equipment at $10,250; he bought equipment costing $3,450 and he sold equipment valued at $2,175. At the end of his financial year he valued his equipment at $8,000.**

What is his depreciation charge on equipment for the year?

A $2,250

B $3,525

C $5,700

D $11,525

188 In the year to 31 December 20X8 Heathside Ltd received £49,200 rental income. The amounts of rent received in advance and due in arrears were as follows

	31 Dec 20X8	*31 Dec 20X7*
	£	£
Rent received in advance	2,400	2,600
Rent due in arrears	1,800	1,400

What figure for rental income should be recorded in the profit and loss account for the year ended 31 December 20X8?

A £48,600

B £49,000

C £49,400

D £49,800

189 An organisation's year end is 30 September. On 1 January 20X6 the organisation took out a loan of £100,000 with annual interest of 12%. The interest is payable in equal instalments on the first day of April, July, October and January in arrears.

How much should be charged to the profit and loss account for the year ended 30 September 20X6, and how much should be accrued on the balance sheet?

	Profit and loss account	*Balance sheet*
A	£12,000	£3,000
B	£9,000	£3,000
C	£9,000	Nil
D	£6,000	£3,000

190 Portals pays a rent bill of £1,800 for the eighteen months ended 30 June 20X9 on 5 May 20X8.

What is the charge to profit and loss and the balance sheet entry for rent in respect of the year ended 31 March 20X9?

A £1,200 with prepayment of £300

B £1,200 with accrual of £600

C £1,500 with accrual of £300

D £1,500 with prepayment of £300

191 What would be the effect on a company's profit of discovering stock with cost of £1,250 and a net realisable value of £1,000, assuming that the same stock had not been included in the original stocktake?

A An increase of £1,250

B An increase of £1,000

C A decrease of £250

D No effect at all

192 **An organisation's stock at 1 July is 15 units at £3.00 each. The following movements occur:**

3 July 20X4	5 units sold at £3.30 each
8 July 20X4	10 units bought at £3.50 each
12 July 20X4	8 units sold at £4.00 each

Closing stock at 31 July, using the FIFO method of stock valuation, would be

A   £31.50

B   £36.00

C   £39.00

D   £41.00

193 **Stationery paid for during 20X5 amounted to £1,350. At the beginning of 20X5 there was a stock of stationery on hand of £165 and an outstanding stationery invoice for £80. At the end of 20X5, there was a stock of stationery on hand of £140 and an outstanding stationery invoice for £70.**

The stationery figure to be shown in the profit and loss account for 20X5 is:

A   £1,195

B   £1,335

C   £1,365

D   £1,505

194 **Rent paid on 1 October 20X2 for the year to 30 September 20X3 was £1,200, and rent paid on 1 October 20X3 for the year to 30 September 20X4 was £1,600.**

Rent payable, as shown in the profit and loss account for the year ended 31 December 20X3, would be:

A   £1,200

B   £1,600

C   £1,300

D   £1,500

195 **Your firm bought a machine for £5,000 on 1 January 20X1, which had an expected useful life of four years and an expected residual value of £1,000; the asset was to be depreciated on the straight-line basis. On 31 December 20X3, the machine was sold for £1,600.**

The amount to be entered in the 20X3 profit and loss account for profit or loss on disposal, is:

A   profit of £600

B   loss of £600

C   profit of £350

D   loss of £400

196 **On 1 July 20X7, your fixed asset register showed a net book value of £47,500. The ledger accounts showed fixed assets at cost of £60,000 and provision for depreciation of £15,000. It was discovered that the disposal of an asset for £4,000, giving rise to a loss on disposal of £1,500, had not been recorded in the fixed asset register.**

After correcting this omission, the fixed asset register would show a balance which was:

A   £3,000 lower than the ledger accounts

B   £1,500 lower than the ledger accounts

C   equal to the ledger accounts

D   £1,000 higher than the ledger accounts.

197 **Your organisation uses the Weighted Average Cost method of valuing stocks. During August 20X7, the following stock details were recorded:**

Opening balance	30 units valued at £2 each
5 August	purchase of 50 units at £2.40 each
8 August	issue of 40 units
18 August	purchase of 60 units at £2.50 each
23 August	issue of 25 units

The value of the balance at 31 August 20X7 was:

A £172.50

B £176.25

C £180.00

D £187.50

198 **A business incurs expenditure on the following research and development activities:**

£120,000 on pure research

£200,000 on applied research

£350,000 on product development

The amount which could be capitalised is:

A nil

B £350,000

C £550,000

D £670,000

199 **A machine cost £9,000. It has an expected useful life of 6 years, and an expected residual value of £1,000. It is to be depreciated at 30% per annum on the reducing balance basis. A full year's depreciation is charged in the year of purchase, with none in the year of sale. During year 4, it is sold for £3,000.**

The profit or loss on disposal is:

A loss £87

B loss £2,000

C profit £256

D profit £1,200

200 **By charging depreciation in the accounts, a business aims to ensure that:**

A the cost of fixed assets is spread over the accounting periods which benefit from their use.

B there are sufficient funds set aside to replace the assets when necessary.

C its profits are not understated.

D the assets are shown at their real value.

201   In times of rising prices, the valuation of stock using the First In First Out method, as opposed to the Weighted Average Cost method, will result in which ONE of the following combinations?

	Cost of sales	Profit	Closing stock
A	Lower	Higher	Higher
B	Lower	Higher	Lower
C	Higher	Lower	Higher
D	Higher	Higher	Lower

202   At the year end of SED Ltd in December 20X0, a journal entry was raised to accrue for utility expenses of $3,600. This journal entry was reversed in January 20X1. During the year ended December 20X1, $30,000 was paid for utility expenses, of which $4,000 was prepaid at the year end.

The charge to the profit and loss account for utility expenses for the year ended December 20X1 was

A $22,400

B $29,600

C $30,400

D $37,600

203   On the first day of Month 1, a business had prepaid insurance of $10,000. On the first day of Month 8, it paid, in full, the annual insurance invoice of $36,000, to cover the following year.

The amount charged in the profit and loss account and the amount shown in the balance sheet at the year end is:

	Profit and loss account $	Balance carried forward $
A	5,000	24,000
B	22,000	23,000
C	25,000	21,000
D	36,000	15,000

204   SSG Ltd bought a machine for $40,000 in January 20X1. The machine had an expected useful life of six years and an expected residual value of $10,000. The machine was depreciated on the straight-line basis. In December 20X4, the machine was sold for $15,000. The company has a policy in its internal accounts of combining the depreciation charge with the profit or loss on disposal of assets.

The total amount of depreciation and profit/loss charged to the internal profit and loss account over the life of the machine was:

A $15,000

B $20,000

C $25,000

D $30,000

205 At the beginning of Period 6, XYZ Ltd had opening stock of 20 units of product X valued at $4·00 each. During Period 6, the following stock movements occurred:

Day 5 Sold 15 items for $5·00 each

Day 10 Bought 8 items for $6·00 each

Day 14 Sold 12 items for $7·00 each

Using the FIFO method of stock valuation, the closing stock at the end of Period 6 was:

A $5.00

B $5.50

C $6.00

D $7.00

PREPARATION OF ACCOUNTS: FINANCIAL STATEMENTS AND RATIO ANALYSIS

206 Which ONE of the following expenses should be included in prime cost in a manufacturing account?

A   Repairs to factory machinery.

B   Direct production wages.

C   Office salaries.

D   Factory insurance.

207 The following information relates to M Ltd:

At 30 September	20X3	20X2
	£000	£000
Stock of raw materials	75	45
Work-in-progress stock	60	70
Stock of finished goods	100	90

For the year ended 30 September 20X3	£000
Purchases of raw materials	150
Manufacturing wages	50
Factory overheads	40

The prime cost of production in the manufacturing account for the year ended 30 September 20X3 is:

A   £165,000.

B   £170,000.

C   £210,000.

D   £270,000.

208 At the end of its financial year, a company has the following fixed assets:

Land and buildings at cost   £10.4 million

Land and buildings: accumulated depreciation   £0.12 million

The company has decided to revalue its land and buildings at the year end to £15 million.

What will be the amount of the transfer to the revaluation reserve?

£	million

209 A business has made a profit of £8,000 but its bank balance has fallen by £5,000. This could be due to:

A   depreciation of £3,000 and an increase in stocks of £10,000

B   depreciation of £6,000 and the repayment of a loan of £7,000

C   depreciation of £12,000 and the purchase of new fixed assets for £25,000

D   the disposal of a fixed asset for £13,000 less than its book value.

210 P does not keep a full set of business records, but the following information is available for the month of June 20X9

	£
Trade debtors, 1 June 20X9	800
Trade debtors, 30 June 20X9	550
Credit sales	6,800
Cash received from debtors	6,730
Bad debt written off	40
General provision for doubtful debts set up at 30 June 20X9	100

Assuming no other transactions, how much discount was allowed to customers during the month?

A   £240

B   £280

C   £340

D   £380

211 From the following information, calculate the value of purchases:

	£
Opening creditors	142,600
Cash paid to suppliers	542,300
Discounts received	13,200
Goods returned	27,500
Closing creditors	137,800

A   £302,600

B   £506,400

C   £523,200

D   £578,200

212 The following information is relevant to the calculation of the sales figure for Alpha, a sole trader who does not keep proper accounting records:

	£
Opening debtors	29,100
Cash received from credit customers and paid into the bank	381,600
Expenses paid out of cash received from credit customers before banking	6,800
Bad debts written off	7,200
Refunds to credit customers	2,100
Discounts allowed to credit customers	9,400
Cash sales	112,900
Closing debtors	38,600

The figure which should appear in Alpha's trading account for sales is:

A   £525,300

B   £511,700

C   £529,500

D   £510,900

213   **A sole trader who does not keep full accounting records wishes to calculate her sales revenue for the year.**

The information available is:

1	Opening stock	£17,000
2	Closing stock	£24,000
3	Purchases	£91,000
4	Standard gross profit percentage on sales revenue:	40%

Which of the following is the sales figure for the year calculated from these figures?

A   £117,600

B   £108,000

C   £210,000

D   £140,000

214   **On 31 December 20X3 the stock of V Limited was completely destroyed by fire.**

The following information is available:

1	Stock at 1 December 20X3 at cost	£28,400
2	Purchases for December 20X3	£49,600
3	Sales for December 20X3	£64,800
4	Standard gross profit percentage on sales revenue	30%

Based on this information, which of the following is the amount of stock destroyed?

£ [   ]

215   **Drab Limited made a profit of £63,200 for the year, after deducting depreciation charges of £15,900 and allowing for a profit of £7,000 on disposal of a fixed asset.**

Fixed asset purchases in the period were £18,000. Debtors increased by £4,000, stocks increased by £3,500 and trade creditors decreased by £1,600.

What was the increase in cash balances during the year?

A   £45,000

B   £48,200

C   £59,000

D   £63,200

216   **There is £100 in the cash till at the year end at F Ltd, but the accountant has discovered that some cash has been stolen.**

At the beginning of the year there was £50 in the cash till and debtors were £2,000. Total sales in the year were £230,000. Debtors at the end of the year were £3,000. Cheques banked from credit sales were £160,000 and cash sales of £50,000 have been banked.

How much cash was stolen during the year?

£ [   ]

217 The following totals appear in the day books for March 20X8:

	Goods excluding VAT	VAT
	£	£
Sales day book	40,000	7,000
Purchases day book	20,000	3,500
Returns outwards day book	2,000	350
Returns inwards day book	4,000	700

The balance of stock, debtors and trade creditors were the same at the end of the month as at the beginning of the month. The gross profit for March 20X8 is:

A £18,000

B £21,150

C £22,000

D £25,850

218 P is a sole proprietor whose accounting records are incomplete. All the sales are cash sales and during the year $50,000 was banked, including $5,000 from the sale of a business car. He paid $12,000 wages in cash from the till and withdrew $2,000 per month as drawings. The cash in the till at the beginning and end of the year was $300 and $400 respectively.

What were the sales for the year?

A $80,900

B $81,000

C $81,100

D $86,100

219 At 1 July 20X3 the share capital and share premium account of a company were as follows:

	£
Share capital – 300,000 ordinary shares of 25p cach	75,000
Share premium account	200,000

During the year ended 30 June 20X4 the following events took place:

1 On 1 January 20X4 the company made a rights issue of one share for every five held, at £1.20 per share.

2 On 1 April 20X4 the company made a bonus (capitalisation) issue of one share for every three in issue at that time, using the share premium account to do so.

What are the correct balances on the company's share capital and share premium accounts at 30 June 20X4?

	Share capital	Share premium account
A	£460,000	£287,000
B	£480,000	£137,000
C	£120,000	£137,000
D	£120,000	£227,000

220 The purchase of a business for more than the aggregate of the fair value of its separable identifiable assets results in the creation of a:

A   share premium account

B   reserve account

C   suspense account

D   goodwill account.

221 A company has £100,000 of ordinary shares at a par value of 10 pence each and 100,000 5% preference shares at a par value of 50 pence each.

The directors decide to declare a dividend of 5p per ordinary share.

The total amount to be paid out in dividends amounts to:

A   £5,000

B   £7,500

C   £52,500

D   £55,000.

222 The correct ledger entries needed to record the issue of 200,000 £1 shares at a premium of 30p, and paid for by cheque, in full, would be:

A   Debit share capital account   £200,000
   Credit share premium account   £60,000
   Credit bank account   £140,000

B   Debit bank account   £260,000
   Credit share capital account   £200,000
   Credit share premium account   £60,000

C   Debit share capital account   £200,000
   Debit share premium account   £60,000
   Credit bank account   £260,000

D   Debit bank account   £200,000
   Debit share premium account   £60,000
   Credit share capital account   £260,000

223 A draft balance sheet has been prepared for Z Ltd. It is now discovered that a loan due for repayment by Z Ltd fourteen months after the balance sheet date has been included in trade creditors.

The necessary adjustment will:

A   have no effect on net current assets

B   increase net current assets

C   reduce net current assets

D   increase current assets but reduce net current assets.

224 Which ONE of the following is an appropriation by a limited company?

A   Directors' salaries.

B   Dividends.

C   Donation to a charity.

D   Loan interest.

225   A business can make a profit and yet have a reduction in its bank balance. Which ONE of the following might cause this to happen?

  A   The sale of fixed assets at a loss.

  B   The charging of depreciation in the profit and loss account.

  C   The lengthening of the period of credit given to customers.

  D   The lengthening of the period of credit taken from suppliers.

226   Which ONE of the following does NOT form part of the equity capital of a limited company?

  A   Preference share capital.

  B   Share premium.

  C   Revaluation reserve.

  D   Ordinary share capital

227   A company's working capital was £43,200. Subsequently, the following transactions occurred:

  •   Creditors were paid £3,000 by cheque.

  •   A bad debt of £250 was written off.

  •   Stock valued at £100 was sold for £230 on credit.

  Working capital is now:

  £

228   A company has an authorised share capital of 1,000,000 ordinary shares of £1 each, of which 800,000 have been issued at a premium of 50p each, thereby raising capital of £1,200,000. The directors are considering allocating £120,000 for dividend payments this year.

  This amounts to a dividend of:

  A   12p per share

  B   10p per share

  C   15p per share

  D   12%.

229   A particular source of finance has the following characteristics: a fixed return, a fixed repayment date, it is secured and the return is classified as an expense.

  Is the source of finance:

  A   ordinary share capital

  B   hire purchase

  C   debenture

  D   preference share?

230 Catch Limited provides the following note to fixed assets in its balance sheet.

Plant and machinery	Cost	Depreciation	Net book value
	£000	£000	£000
Opening balance	453	143	310
Additions/charge	102	11	91
Disposals	(79)	(64)	(15)
Closing balance	476	90	386

The additional machinery was purchased for cash. The disposals were made at a loss of £6,000.

What was the net cash outflow on plant and machinery during the period?

£ _____

231 The movement on the plant and machinery account for X Ltd is shown below:

	£
Cost b/fwd	10,000
Additions	2,000
Disposals	(3,000)
Cost c/fwd	9,000
Depreciation b/fwd	2,000
Charge for the year	1,000
Disposals	(1,500)
Depreciation c/fwd	1,500
Net book value b/fwd	8,000
Net book value c/fwd	7,500

The profit on the sale of the machine was £500. What figures would appear in the cash flow statement of X Ltd?

A   Movement on plant account £500 and profit on disposal of £500.

B   Movement on plant account £500 and proceeds on sale of plant £2,000.

C   Purchase of plant £2,000 and profit on disposal of £500.

D   Purchase of plant £2,000 and proceeds on sale of plant £2,000.

232 Extracts from the financial statements of CFS Ltd are set out below:

Profit and loss account for the year ended 31 December 20X1

	£000	£000
Turnover		300
Cost of sales		150
Gross profit		150
Profit on sale of fixed asset		75
		225
Expenses	15	
Depreciation	30	
		45
Net profit		180

	Balances at 31 December	
	20X0	20X1
	£000	£000
Stock, debtors, current liabilities (net)	40	50

What figure, in £000, would appear for cash in the cash flow statement of CFS Ltd for the year ended 31 December 20X1 in respect of net cash flow from operating activities?

A   £125

B   £145

C   £215

D   £235

233   **In relation to cash flow statements, which, if any, of the following are correct?**

Statement

1   The direct method of calculating net cash from operating activities leads to a different figure from that produced by the indirect method, but this is balanced elsewhere in the cash flow statement.

2   A company making high profits must necessarily have a net cash inflow from operating activities.

3   Profits and losses on disposals of fixed assets appear as items under capital expenditure in the cash flow statement or a note to it.

A   Statement 1 only

B   Statement 2 only

C   Statement 3 only

D   None of the statements

234   **A cash flow statement prepared in accordance with the indirect method reconciles operating profit to net operating cash flow.**

Which of the following lists of items consists only of items that would be ADDED to operating profit in that note?

A   Decrease in stock, depreciation, profit on sale of fixed assets.

B   Increase in creditors, decrease in debtors, profit on sale of fixed assets.

C   Loss on sale of fixed assets, depreciation, increase in debtors.

D   Decrease in debtors, increase in creditors, loss on sale of fixed assets.

235 **Information about the fixed assets of Rabbit Limited is as follows.**

	£000
Net book value at 1 January 20X4	2,400
Net book value at 31 December 20X4	6,000
Net book value of fixed assets disposed of during 20X4	500
Depreciation charge for the year ending 31 December 20X4	1,000
Loss arising on disposal of fixed assets during 20X4	150

What will be the figures for fixed asset disposals and fixed asset additions in the cash flow statement for the year to 31 December 20X4?

Disposals	£
Additions	£

236 **A company made a profit for the year of £18,750, after accounting for depreciation of £1,250.**

During the year, fixed assets were purchased for £8,000, debtors increased by £1,000, stocks decreased by £1,800 and creditors increased by £350.

The increase in cash and bank balances during the year was:

A   £10,650

B   £10,850

C   £12,450

D   £13,150.

237 **The formula for calculating the rate of stock turnover is:**

A   average stock at cost divided by cost of goods sold

B   sales divided by average stock at cost

C   sales divided by average stock at selling price

D   cost of goods sold divided by average stock at cost.

238 **A company has the following current assets and liabilities at 31 October 20X8:**

		£000
Current assets:	stock	970
	debtors	380
	bank	40
		1,390
Current liabilities:	creditors	420

When measured against accepted 'norms', the company can be said to have:

A   a high current ratio and an ideal acid test ratio

B   an ideal current ratio and a low acid test ratio

C   a high current ratio and a low acid test ratio

D   ideal current and acid test ratios.

239 An analysis of its financial statements revealed that the debtor collection period of R Limited was 100 days, when 60 days is a reasonable figure.

Which one of the following could NOT account for the high level of 100 days?

A   Poor performance in R's credit control department

B   A large credit sale made just before the balance sheet date

C   R's trade is seasonal

D   A downturn in R's trade in the last quarter of the year

240 The analysis of a company's financial statements revealed that the number of days' sales in stock was 80 days. The average for companies in the same industry was 35 days.

Which of the following is LEAST likely to account for the high level of 80 days?

A   The company's trade is seasonal

B   Poor stock control

C   A large purchase was made just before the balance sheet date

D   An increase in the company's sales in the three months before the balance sheet date

241 Which of the following correctly defines working capital?

A   Fixed assets plus current assets minus current liabilities

B   Current assets minus current liabilities

C   Fixed assets plus current assets

D   Share capital plus reserves

The following data relates to Questions 242 and 243.

Extracts from a company's financial statements for the year ended 30 September 20X1 are given below.

Balance sheet	£000	Profit and loss account	£000
Issued share capital	500	Operating profit	300
Share premium	200	Interest payable	100
Profit and loss account	800	Profit before tax	200
Non-current liabilities:			
10% debentures	1,000		

242 What is the return on shareholders' equity as a percentage, based on these figures?

A   40%

B   20%

C   13.3%

D   12%

243 What is the return on total capital employed as a percentage, based on these figures?

A   12%

B   8%

C   13.3%

D   20%

244 You are given the following extract from a company's profit and loss account.

	£000
Turnover	15,000
Opening stock at cost	1,750
Purchases	10,200
Closing stock at cost	1,950

Assuming continuity in the rate of turnover, how many days' worth of sales does the business have in stock at the year-end (to the nearest day)?

A 47 days

B 68 days

C 70 days

D 71 days

245 Mr Worthing expects that his business will have net current liabilities at the financial year-end. The raising of extra funds on a short term loan at the balance sheet date would:

A improve the current ratio

B worsen the current ratio

C have no effect on the current ratio

D either improve or worsen the current ratio depending upon the balances involved and the extra funds raised.

246 George Bentley discovers that his business has made a loss during the financial year just ended, but that it has more cash at the end of the year than it did at the beginning.

Which of the following could be a reason for this?

A George drew more out of the business this year than last

B Some fixed assets were sold during the year

C Debtors took longer to pay this year than last

D Prepayments were higher at the end of this year

247 The net profit percentage in a company is 12% and the asset turnover ratio is 2.

What is the return on capital employed?

A 6%

B 10%

C 14%

D 24%

248 A summary of the balance sheet of M Ltd at 31 March 20X2 was as follows:

	£000
Total assets less current liabilities	120
Ordinary share capital	40
Share premium account	10
Profit and loss account	10
5% debentures 2010	60
	120

If the operating profit for the year ended 31 March 20X2 was £15,000, what is the return on capital employed?

A 12.5 per cent.

B 25 per cent.

C 30 per cent.

D 37.5 per cent.

249 The annual sales of a company are £235,000 including VAT at 17.5 per cent. Half of the sales are on credit terms; half are cash sales. The debtors in the balance sheet are £23,500.

What are the debtor days (to the nearest day)?

A 37 days

B 43 days

C 73 days

D 86 days

250 The draft balance sheet of B Ltd at 31 March 20X3 is set out below.

	£	£
Fixed assets		450
Current assets		
Stock	65	
Debtors	110	
Prepayments	30	
	205	
Current liabilities		
Creditors	30	
Bank overdraft (Note 1)	50	
	80	
		125
		575
Long-term liability:		
Loan		(75)
		500
Ordinary share capital		400
Profit and loss account		100
		500

Note: The bank overdraft first occurred on 30 September 20X2.

What is the gearing of the company?

A 13 per cent

B 16 per cent

C 20 per cent

D 24 per cent

251 An increase in stock of £250, a decrease in the bank balance of £400 and an increase in creditors of £1,200 result in:

A a decrease in working capital of £1,350

B an increase in working capital of £1,350

C a decrease in working capital of £1,050

D an increase in working capital of £1,050.

252 Working capital will reduce by £500 if:

    A   goods costing £3,000 are sold for £3,500 on credit

    B   goods costing £3,000 are sold for £3,500 cash

    C   fixed assets costing £500 are purchased on credit

    D   fixed assets with a net book value of £750 are sold for £250 cash.

253 From the following information regarding the year to 31 August 20X6, what is the creditors' payment period?

	£
Sales	43,000
Cost of sales	32,500
Opening stock	6,000
Closing stock	3,800
Creditors at 31 August 20X6	4,750

    A   40 days

    B   50 days

    C   53 days

    D   57 days

254 During the year ended 31 October 20X7, your organisation made a gross profit of £60,000, which represented a mark-up of 50%. Opening stock was £12,000 and closing stock was £18,000.

The rate of stock turnover was:

    A   4 times

    B   6.7 times

    C   7.3 times

    D   8 times.

255 A business operates on a gross profit margin of $33\frac{1}{3}$%. Gross profit on a sale was £800, and expenses were £680.

The net profit percentage is:

    A   3.75%

    B   5%

    C   11.25%

    D   22.67%.

256 A business has the following trading account for the year ending 31 May 20X8:

	£	£
Sales turnover		45,000
Opening stock	4,000	
Purchases	26,500	
	30,500	
Less: Closing stock	6,000	
		24,500
Gross profit		20,500

Its rate of stock turnover for the year is:

A   4.9 times

B   5.3 times

C   7.5 times

D   9 times.

257   A company has the following details extracted from its balance sheet:

	£000
Stocks	1,900
Debtors	1,000
Bank overdraft	100
Creditors	1,000

Its liquidity position could be said to be:

A   very well-controlled because its current assets far outweigh its current liabilities

B   poorly-controlled because its quick assets are less than its current liabilities

C   poorly-controlled because its current ratio is significantly higher than the industry norm of 1.8

D   poorly-controlled because it has a bank overdraft.

258   The gearing ratio is often calculated as:

A   long-term loans as a percentage of total shareholders' funds

B   current and long-term debt as a percentage of total net assets

C   long-term loans and preference shares as a percentage of total shareholders' funds

D   preference shares as a percentage of equity capital.

259   An increase in the gross profit margin of a business is most likely to be due to which ONE of the following combinations:

	Selling price per unit	Quantity sold	Cost per unit
A	increased	no change	increased
B	no change	increased	no change
C	no change	no change	decreased
D	decreased	increased	increased

260   A business has the following capital and long-term liabilities:

	31.10.X3 £million	31.10.X4 £million
8% Debentures	15	50
Issued share capital	20	30
Share premium	10	20
Retained profits	43	36

At 31 October 20X4, its gearing ratio, compared to that at 31 October 20X3, has:

A   risen, resulting in greater risk for shareholders

B   risen, resulting in greater security for shareholders

C   fallen, resulting in greater security for shareholders

D   remained the same.

261   A business has the following trading accounts:

	Year ended 31 October 20X8		Year ended 31 October 20X9	
	£000	£000	£000	£000
Sales		2,000		2,650
Less: Cost of sales				
Opening stock	75		85	
Purchases	1,260		1,330	
	1,335		1,415	
Less: Closing stock	85		115	
		1,250		1,300
Gross profit		750		1,350

During the year ended 31 October 20X9, its rate of stock turnover, compared with that for the year ended 31 October 20X8, has:

A   decreased, with a possible beneficial effect on liquidity

B   decreased, with a possible detrimental effect on liquidity

C   increased, with a possible detrimental effect on liquidity

D   increased, with a possible beneficial effect on liquidity.

262   The M Club discloses the following note to its Income and Expenditure Account:

'Subscriptions in arrears are accounted for when received; subscriptions in advance are accounted for on a matching basis.'

At 31 March 20X1, there were subscriptions owing of $1,000 and subscriptions in advance of $500.

During the year ended 31 March 20X2, subscriptions of $10,000 were received, including subscriptions relating to the previous year of $800 and subscriptions in advance of $600.

What amount should be included for subscriptions in the year ended 31 March 20X2?

A $8,100

B $8,900

C $9,100

D $9,900

263   The following information at 5 January 20X2 related to a club, which has a year end of 31 December 20X1:

	$
Subscriptions for 20X0 unpaid at January 20X1	300
Subscriptions for 20X0 paid during the year ended 31 December 20X1	250
Subscriptions for 20X1 paid during the year ended 31 December 20X1	6,000
Subscriptions for 20X2 paid during the year ended 31 December 20X1	1,000
Subscriptions for 20X1 unpaid at 31 December 20X1	750

It is the club's policy to write off overdue subscriptions after one year.

What amount should be credited to the income and expenditure account for the year ended 31 December 20X1?

A $6,250

B $6,750

C $7,050

D $7,250

264 The difference between a profit and loss account (which may also be referred to as an 'income statement') and an income and expenditure account is that:

A   an income and expenditure account is an international term for a profit and loss account.

B   a profit and loss account is prepared for a business and an income and expenditure account is prepared for a not-for-profit making organisation.

C   a profit and loss account is prepared on an accruals basis and an income and expenditure account is prepared on a cash flow basis.

D   a profit and loss account is prepared for a manufacturing business and an income and expenditure account is prepared for a non-manufacturing business.

265 The Almondsbury Social Club takes credit for subscriptions when due. The register of members totalled 1,548 at 31 December 20X8, of which twenty-five had still to pay their subscriptions, whilst seventy-two had paid in advance for the following year. At the beginning of the year fifty-two members had yet to pay their subscriptions for 20X7 whilst twenty-seven had paid in advance for 20X8.

If the annual subscription was £8 in 20X7, £10 in 20X8 and £12 in 20X9, what was received from members in the year ended 31 December 20X8?

A   £14,720

B   £15,480

C   £16,204

D   £16,240

266 The policy of the Stapenhill Social Club is to take credit for members' subscriptions as they become due. For the year ended 30 September 20X8, on which date subscriptions were due, 1,200 members were on the register, of whom 15 had paid their subscriptions in advance, whilst 18 were in arrears at the beginning of the year.

If the annual subscription is £12, 17 members had paid their subscriptions for the year ended 30 September 20X9 in advance, and £14,640 had been banked during the year, how many members are in arrears with their subscriptions at 30 September 20X8?

A   None

B   17

C   34

D   40

267 A club received subscriptions during 20X5 totalling £12,500. Of these, £800 related to 20X4 and £400 related to 20X6. There were subscriptions in arrears at the end of 20X5 of £250. The subscriptions to be included in the Income and Expenditure account for 20X5 amount to:

A   £11,050

B   £11,550

C   £11,850

D   £12,350

268 An income and expenditure account is:

A   a summary of the cash and bank transactions for a period

B   another name for a receipts and payments account

C   similar to a profit and loss account in reflecting revenue earned and expenses incurred during a period

D   a balance sheet as prepared for a non-profit making organisation.

269 **Life membership fees payable to a club are usually dealt with by:**

A   crediting the total received to a life membership fees account and transferring a proportion each year to the income and expenditure account

B   crediting the total received to the income and expenditure account in the year in which these fees are received

C   debiting the total received to a life membership fees account and transferring a proportion each year to the income and expenditure account

D   debiting the total received to the income and expenditure account in the year in which these fees are received.

270 **A club's membership fees account shows a debit balance of £150 and a credit balance of £90 at 1 June 20X7. During the year ending 31 May 20X8, subscriptions received amounted to £4,750. Subscriptions overdue from the year ended 31 May 20X7, of £40, are to be written off. At 31 May 20X8, subscriptions paid in advance amount to £75.**

The amount to be transferred to the income and expenditure account for the year ending 31 May 20X8 is:

A   £4,575

B   £4,655

C   £4,775

D   £4,875

271 **The subscriptions receivable account of a club commenced the year with subscriptions in arrears of £50 and subscriptions in advance of £75. During the year, £12,450 was received in subscriptions, including all of the arrears and £120 for next year's subscriptions.**

The amount to be taken to the income and expenditure account for the year is:

A   £12,205

B   £12,355

C   £12,545

D   £12,595

272 **The accumulated fund represents:**

A   the total of the shareholders' investment in a company.

B   the book value of net assets in a not-for-profit organisation.

C   the excess of income over expenditure in a not-for-profit organisation.

D   the bank balances of an organisation.

273 **The following information relates to Hanford Ltd for the year ended 30 September 20X9**

	£000
Turnover	300
Purchases	230
Opening stock	55

The company operates at a uniform mark-up of 20% on cost price.

The closing stock amounts to:

A   £35,000

B   £45,000

C   £65,000

D   £75,000

274   **Many of the records of G Ltd have been destroyed by fire. The following information is available for the period under review.**

(i)   Sales totalled £480,000.

(ii)   Stock at cost was opening £36,420, closing £40,680.

(iii) Trade creditors were opening £29,590, closing £33,875.

(iv)   Gross profit for the period should represent a mark-up on cost of 50%.

What was the total for the period of cash paid to suppliers?

A   £239,975

B   £315,715

C   £319,975

D   £328,545

275   **A manufacturer has the following figures for the year ended 30 September 20X6:**

	£
Direct materials	8,000
Factory overheads	12,000
Direct labour	10,000
Increase in work-in-progress	4,000

Prime cost is:

A   £18,000

B   £26,000

C   £30,000

D   £34,000

276   **Gross profit for 20X3 can be calculated from:**

A   purchases for 20X3, plus stock at 31 December 20X3, less stock at 1 January 20X3.

B   purchases for 20X3, less stock at 31 December 20X3, plus stock at 1 January 20X3.

C   cost of goods sold during 20X3, plus sales during 20X3.

D   net profit for 20X3, plus expenses for 20X3.

277   **You are given the following information:**

Debtors at 1 January 20X3	£10,000
Debtors at 31 December 20X3	£9,000
Total receipts during 20X3 (including cash sales of £5,000)	£85,000

Sales on credit during 20X3 amount to:

A   £81,000

B   £86,000

C   £79,000

D   £84,000

278 Your company sells goods on 29 December 20X3, on sale or return; the final date for return or payment in full is 10 January 20X4. The costs of manufacturing the product are all incurred and paid for in 20X3 except for an outstanding bill for carriage outwards which is still unpaid.

The associated revenues and expenses of the transaction should be dealt with in the profit and loss account by:

A   including all revenues and all expenses in 20X3.

B   including all revenues and all expenses in 20X4.

C   including expenses in 20X3 and revenues in 20X4.

D   including the revenue and the carriage outwards in 20X4, and the other expenses in 20X3.

279 A business has opening stock of £12,000 and closing stock of £18,000. Purchase returns were £5,000. The cost of goods sold was £111,000.

Purchases were:

A   £100,000

B   £110,000

C   £116,000

D   £122,000

280 An increase in the figure for work-in-progress will:

A   increase the prime cost

B   decrease the prime cost

C   increase the cost of goods sold

D   decrease the factory cost of goods completed.

The following information is required for questions 281 to 282

The accounts for SPA plc are set out below.

Profit and loss account
for the year ended 30 November 20X2

	$000	$000
Turnover		5,000
Opening stock	200	
Purchases	3,100	
Closing stock	(300)	
Cost of sales		(3,000)
Gross profit		2,000
Operating expenses		(500)
Operating profit		1,500

Balance sheet at 30 November 20X2

	$000	$000
Fixed assets		3,000
Current assets		
Stock	300	
Debtors	900	
Bank	50	
	1,250	
Current liabilities		
Trade creditors	(250)	
		1,000
		4,000
Share capital		2,000
Profit and loss account		2,000
		4,000

281 **The return on capital employed in SPA plc is:**

A 75.0%

B 37.5%

C 50.0%

D 100.0%

282 **The fixed asset turnover ratio in SPA plc is:**

A 1 : 1.67

B 1.25 : 1

C 2.5 : 1

D 1.67 : 1

283 **The quick ratio (acid test ratio) In SPA plc is:**

A 2.4 : 1

B 3.8 : 1

C 4.8 : 1

D 5.1 : 1

284 The year end for ABC Ltd is July 20X2 and in that month a company car was stolen. The net book value of the company car was $8,000, but the company expects the insurance company to pay only $6,000. The correct journal entry to record this information was entered in the books in July 20X2. In August 20X2 the insurance company sent a cheque for $6,500.

The journal entry to record this is:

			Dr $	Cr $
A	Bank		6,500	
		Sundry debtor		6,500
B	Bank		6,500	
		Sundry debtor		6,000
		Disposal of fixed assets account		500
C	Bank		500	
		Disposal of fixed assets account		500
D	Bank		500	
		Sundry debtor		500

285 At the beginning of the year in GHI Ltd, the opening work-in-progress was $240,000.

During the year, the following expenditure was incurred:

Prime cost: $720,000

Factory overheads: $72,000

The closing work-in-progress was $350,000

The factory cost of goods completed during the year was:

A $538,000

B $610,000

C $682,000

D $902,000

Section 2

PRACTICE QUESTIONS

CONCEPTUAL AND REGULATORY FRAMEWORK

1   D

D has been an accountant for many years. He had always understood that the historical cost convention was important in the preparation of the financial statements. However, he has recently been attending a series of lectures on accounting and many of the speakers have referred to a move to current cost accounting. He is keen to update his knowledge and has asked you to explain some terms to him.

Required:

(i)	Define 'historical cost accounting'.	**(3 marks)**
(ii)	Give an example to illustrate the use of historical cost accounting.	**(2 marks)**
(iii)	Define 'net realisable value'.	**(2 marks)**
(iv)	Give an example to illustrate the use of net realisable value.	**(2 marks)**
(v)	Define 'current cost accounting'.	**(2 marks)**
(vi)	Define 'economic value'.	**(3 marks)**
(vii)	Explain the effect on historical cost profit and asset values if current cost accounting is used rather than historical cost accounting, assuming rising prices.	**(3 marks)**
(viii)	Define 'capital maintenance'.	**(3 marks)**

(Maximum of 30 words for each explanation)

2   BUSINESS WORLD

The business world encompasses many forms of business organisation.

Required:

(a)   Tick all boxes that apply.

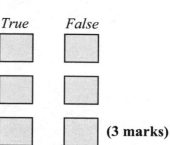

	True	*False*
Corporations, partnerships and sole traders are all forms of business entities.	☐	☐
For accounting purposes, the individual business is **not** regarded as an entity in its own right.	☐	☐
A registered company has a separate legal personality.	☐	☐ **(3 marks)**

(b)   Give three examples of **external** users of financial statements.

(3 marks)

(c)   Complete the missing words in the following.

   (i)   Financial accounting concerns the production of the main _____ mainly for _____ users.   **(2 marks)**

   (ii)   Management accounting concerns the production of mainly for _____ users.   **(2 marks)**

   (iii)   The _____ reflects the performance of a company over a period. It shows the _____ between the position at the beginning and at the close of the period.   **(2 marks)**

   (iv)   Current liabilities are amounts _____ by the business, payable within _____ of the balance sheet date.   **(2 marks)**

   (v)   Capital expenditure is expenditure on acquiring _____ assets. Revenue expenditure is expenditure on items of _____   **(2 marks)**

3   GAAP

Required:

(a)   What does GAAP stand for?

(2 marks)

(b)   Explain the following GAAP principles: *(Each explanation must not exceed 20 words.)*

   (i)   The non-aggregation principle   **(2 marks)**

   (ii)   Substance over form   **(2 marks)**

   (iii)   Materiality   **(2 marks)**

   (iv)   Realisation   **(2 marks)**

   (v)   Relevance   **(2 marks)**

   (vi)   Objectivity   **(2 marks)**

   (vii)   Duality   **(2 marks)**

   (viii)   Money measurement   **(2 marks)**

   (ix)   Stewardship   **(2 marks)**

4   CONCEPTS

Required:

Define the following concepts: *(Your answer for each definition must not exceed 25 words.)*

   (i)   Prudence   **(2 marks)**

   (ii)   Realisation   **(2 marks)**

(iii) Stewardship   **(2 marks)**

(iv) True and fair view   **(2 marks)**

(v) Neutrality   **(2 marks)**

(vi) Money measurement   **(2 marks)**

(vii) Accruals   **(2 marks)**

(viii) Consistency   **(2 marks)**

5 DEFINITIONS

Required:

(a) Define the following four terms in no more than 30 words each.

(i) Asset   **(2 marks)**

(ii) Liability   **(2 marks)**

(iii) Capital receipt   **(2 marks)**

(iv) Capital expenditure   **(2 marks)**

(b) Give an example of each of the four terms you have defined above and explain why it conforms to your definition in no more than 30 words each.

(i) Asset   **(3 marks)**

(ii) Liability   **(3 marks)**

(iii) Capital receipt   **(3 marks)**

(iv) Capital expenditure   **(3 marks)**

ACCOUNTING SYSTEMS

6 TANWIR

Tanwir commenced in business on 1 October 20X9, with capital in the bank of £20,000. During his first month of trading, his transactions were as follows:

2 October	purchased stocks for £3,500 on credit from A Jones
3 October	paid £1,200 rental of premises, by cheque
5 October	paid £5,000 for office equipment, by cheque
10 October	sold goods costing £1,000, for £1,750, on credit to P Duncan
15 October	returned stocks costing £500 to A Jones
18 October	purchased stocks for £2,400 on credit from A Jones
25 October	paid A Jones for the net purchases of 2 October, by cheque
28 October	P Duncan paid £500 on account, by cheque

Required:

Marks are awarded for completing the gaps where a mark (in brackets) is indicated. There are no marks for completing the missing words or figures where no mark is indicated but these will help you to obtain the correct answers.

(a)   Complete the following ledger accounts for the above transactions. Balance off the accounts of A Jones, P Duncan and the bank account at 31 October 20X9, showing clearly the balances brought forward to the next month. (Ignore VAT).   **(13 marks)**

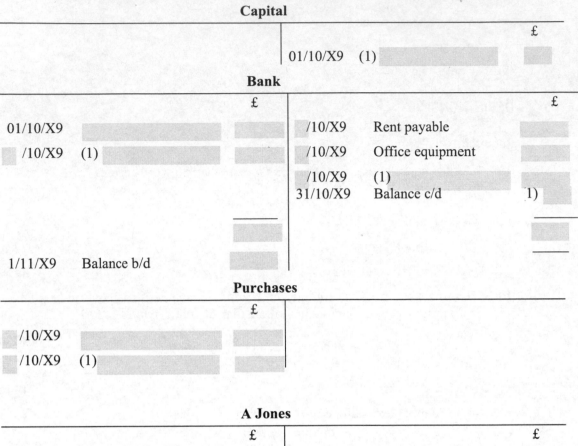

Capital

		£
	01/10/X9 (1)	

Bank

		£				£
01/10/X9			/10/X9	Rent payable		
/10/X9 (1)			/10/X9	Office equipment		
			/10/X9 (1)			
			31/10/X9	Balance c/d		1)
1/11/X9	Balance b/d					

Purchases

		£
/10/X9		
/10/X9 (1)		

A Jones

		£				£
/10/X9 (1)			10/X9 (1)			
/10/X9	Bank	3,000	10/X9	Purchases		2,400
/10/X9	Balance c/d	(1)				
			11/X9	Balance b/d		

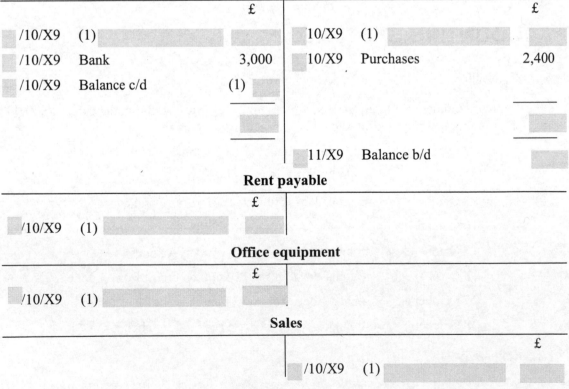

Rent payable

		£
/10/X9 (1)		

Office equipment

		£
/10/X9 (1)		

Sales

		£
	/10/X9 (1)	

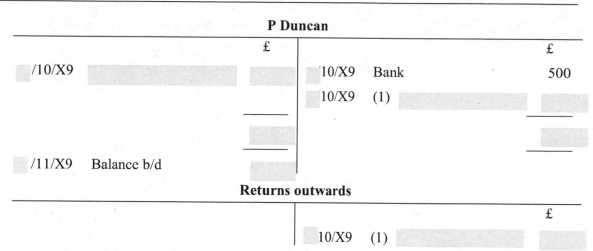

P Duncan

	£			£
/10/X9		10/X9	Bank	500
		10/X9	(1)	
/11/X9 Balance b/d				

Returns outwards

		£
10/X9	(1)	

7 BOOKS OF PRIME ENTRY

(a) Complete the missing words or figures in the following.

(i) _____ discounts are adjustments between the stated price on the price list and the actual price being charged.

(ii) _____ discounts are percentage allowances made to a debtor as an incentive to settle within the terms of the original scale. **(2 marks)**

(b) Tick all boxes that apply.

		True	False
(i)	Trade discounts are recorded in the cash book.	☐	☐
(ii)	Cash discounts are recorded in the cash book.	☐	☐
(iii)	The debtors' and creditors' ledgers form part of the double entry system.	☐	☐
(iv)	The journal book is a book of prime entry.	☐	☐
(v)	The day books are not part of the double entry system.	☐	☐

(vi) A debtors' ledger control account may contain the following totals for the period:

	True	False
- Sales (sales day book)	☐	☐
- Cash paid (cash book)	☐	☐
- Discounts received (cash book)	☐	☐
- Discounts allowed (cash book)	☐	☐
- Sales returns	☐	☐
- Bad debts expense	☐	☐

(11 marks)

8 EMPLOYEES

You are the payroll administrator in your organisation, and your responsibilities include the preparation of the monthly payroll for 100 employees.

Each employee is paid a basic monthly wage, with overtime at time-and-a-third. Employees complete an Overtime Report Form which they submit direct to you each month. You input the necessary data to a computerised payroll system, in batches, which are processed as a single run at the end of each month.

The system produces a monthly summary of payroll data. You then journalise the totals to provide input to the nominal ledger.

You make out cheques in the following month for employees' net wages.

The highest paid employee earns £2,000 basic pay per month gross.

An extract from the payroll printout for the month ended 31 October 20X8 was as follows:

Employee number	Gross wages	Tax	Employee's National Insurance	Pension payments	Employer's National Insurance
	£	£	£	£	£
1	6,000	1,000	200	360	520
2	2,222	360	200	132	160
3	2,160	340	180	125	150
4	1,760	300	160	105	120
↓	↓	↓	↓	↓	↓
↓	↓	↓	↓	↓	↓
100	600	72	48	40	60
Totals	78,000	12,800	5,600	4,600	5,250

Required:

Marks are awarded for completing the gaps where a mark (in brackets) is indicated. There are no marks for completing the missing words or figures where no mark is indicated but these will help you to obtain the correct answers.

(a)   Complete the following journal entries for the above payroll, to be input to the nominal ledger.   (*Note*: Narratives are NOT required.)

		Dr	Cr
Dr	Total wages account	(1)	
Cr	PAYE creditor account		(1)
Cr	NI creditor account		(1)
Cr	Pension scheme creditor account		(1)
Cr	Wage creditor account		(1)

(5 marks)

(b)   State the amount to be debited to the profit and loss account for the month of October, in respect of wages costs, AND show the balance sheet extract for the remaining balances.

The amount to be debited to the profit and loss account for October is

The balance sheet extract at 31 October 20X8 is:

Creditors: (1)

	£
PAYE creditor	
NI creditor	
Pension fund creditor	
Accrued wages	(1)
	(1)

(3 marks)

(c)   Complete the missing words in the comments on THREE possible weaknesses in the administrative controls which exist in the present system.

There appears to be no division of ▨▨▨▨▨ in the payroll department. Your duties as payroll administrator include preparing the payroll, receiving the overtime claim forms, inputting the data and making out the cheques. The opportunity for fraud such as ▨▨▨▨▨ is therefore huge. There should be some division of labour introduced which could be done fairly easily by at the very least the cheques being prepared by another department such as the purchases ledger or the cashier.

The computer should have some form of ▨▨▨▨▨ checks for data that is obviously suspect. For example on this computer printout employee 1 has a gross wage of £6,000 which would be impossible with a maximum basic pay of £2,000 per month. The computer should be able to produce some sort of ▨▨▨▨▨ report highlighting any such figures.

There appears to be little control over overtime payments as the Overtime Report Form is submitted directly to you. An ▨▨▨▨▨ person should firstly authorise any overtime that is to be worked and the hours submitted on the Report Form should be checked to ▨▨▨▨▨ or job sheets.   **(6 marks)**

(d)   Complete the missing words in the description of the operation of batch processing.

A batch processing system is where ▨▨▨▨▨ types of documents are collected together, such as sales invoices or in this case payroll details, and they are then input into the computer in ▨▨▨▨▨. The data is then used by the computer to update the relevant ledger accounts.

Any such input of data should have a number of controls associated with it known as ▨▨▨▨▨ controls. These include the ▨▨▨▨▨ numbering of the documents which does appear to have happened here, each employee is given a sequential number. Prior to input there should also be a batch total calculated and batch header filled in. It is not possible to tell whether this has taken place.

However it is quite clear from the data for employee 1 that there is no procedure within the system. A ▨▨▨▨▨ procedure should check that the input is reasonable by comparing to ▨▨▨▨▨ limits, that the data is current and that the accounts being updated do in fact exist.   **(6 marks)**

CONTROL OF ACCOUNTING SYSTEMS

9   BH

BH commenced in business some years ago, maintaining a single ledger for all accounts, plus a cash book. His business has now expanded to the extent that he now needs to consider improving his accounting system by dividing the ledger into sections and introducing a petty cash system.

Required:

(a)   Complete the missing words or phrases below.

(1) ▨▨▨▨▨ is the actual cash that a business will have on its premises in order to meet small non-cheque payments by employees such as ▨▨▨▨▨.

An (1) ▨▨▨▨▨ system is where a predetermined amount of cash, say £100, is withdrawn from the business' bank account and put into the petty cash box in order to cover the following week's expenses. If an employee wishes to be reimbursed for cash that he has paid out on behalf of the business then that employee must fill out a pre-numbered (1) ▨▨▨▨▨▨▨▨ . Usually this voucher must also be supported by an invoice or receipt. The voucher must then be authorised by the appropriate person and then the employee will be reimbursed out of the petty cash box. The voucher will remain in the petty cash box. Therefore at any point in time the cash in the petty cash box and the vouchers should always total back to the imprest amount, in our case £100.

At the end of the week the total of the vouchers is determined and this amount is then withdrawn from the bank in cash in order to return the petty cash box to the (1) ▨▨▨▨▨▨ amount of £100.

The petty cash expenditure is recorded in the petty cash book from each of the vouchers. The amount of cash paid into the petty cash box to bring it back to the (1) ▨▨▨▨▨▨ amount is also recorded as a receipt in the petty cash book.

The main purpose of the imprest system is therefore to provide (1) ▨▨▨▨▨ over the cash held and to provide a means of reimbursing employees for cash expenditure on behalf of the business. **(6 marks)**

(b)   (i)   Which ledger accounts are debited and credited with the purchases day book totals?

         Debit   ▨▨▨▨▨▨   **(1 mark)**

         Credit   ▨▨▨▨▨▨   **(1 mark)**

   (ii)   Which ledger accounts are debited and credited with the sales day book totals?

         Debit   ▨▨▨▨▨▨   **(1 mark)**

         Credit   ▨▨▨▨▨▨   **(1 mark)**

   (iii)   Where is each individual invoice to customers recorded?

         ▨▨▨▨▨▨ ledger   **(1 mark)**

   (iv)   Where is each individual invoice from suppliers recorded?

         ▨▨▨▨▨▨ ledger   **(1 mark)**

(c)   From the following information, complete the following sales ledger control account for the month of February 20X7:

	£
Owing by customers at 1 February 20X7	103,670
Owing to customers at 1 February 20X7	1,400
Sales, excluding VAT	175,860
VAT on sales	10,350
Returns inwards, including VAT	9,500
VAT on returns inwards	1,300
Refunds to customers	800
Cash sales, including VAT	12,950
Cheques received from debtors	126,750
Discounts allowed to customers	1,150
Contra entries to purchase ledger	750
Bad debts written off	2,300
Dishonoured cheques from debtors	1,580

In addition, BH has been notified that he will receive a dividend of 10p in the £ from a previously written-off bad debt of £3,000. The amount has not yet been received.

At 28 February 20X7, a provision for doubtful bad debts is to be made of 2% of the net balance which existed at 1 February 20X7.

Amounts owing to customers at 28 February 20X7 amounted to £840.

Marks are awarded for completing the gaps where a mark (in brackets) is indicated.
There are no marks for completing the missing words or figures where no mark is
indicated but these will help you to obtain the correct answers.

BH – Sales ledger control account

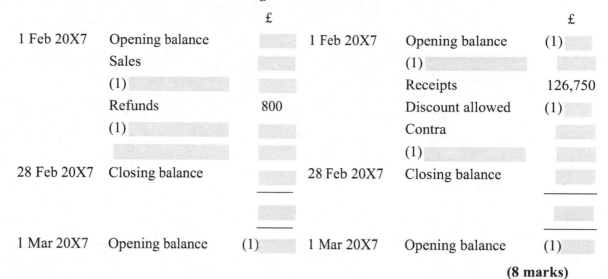

(8 marks)

10 MLN

The trial balance of MLN plc was extracted on 30 September 20X9 and showed the following totals.

> Debit   £1,605,668   Credit   £1,603,623

A suspense account was opened and used to record the difference until it could be investigated but the company continued its draft accounts by applying the prudence concept to the treatment of the suspense account balance.

After investigation the following facts emerged.

(1)   Discounts allowed of £1,248 had not been entered in the sales ledger control account.

(2)   A credit sale of £857 to SEC Ltd had not been entered in the sales day book.

(3)   A contra entry between the sales and purchase ledgers had been entered in the control account as:

> Debit sales ledger control   £731
> Credit purchase ledger control   £731

(4)   A telephone bill of £54 had been entered in the telephone expense account as £45 but was correctly entered in the creditor's account.

(5)   Bank charges of £66 had been correctly entered in the expense account but had not been entered in the cash book.

(6)   One of the pages of the purchase day book had been incorrectly totalled as £11,269 instead of £11,629.

(7)   During the year a fixed asset was sold for £740. Its original cost was £3,600 and its net book value at the date of disposal was £800. The only entry made was to debit the proceeds of sale to the bank account.

Required:

(a)   Complete the missing words and figures in the following suspense account to correct
(1) to (7) above.

*Marks are awarded for completing the gaps where a mark (in brackets) is indicated.
There are no marks for completing the missing words or figures where no mark is
indicated but these will help you to obtain the correct answers.*

Suspense account

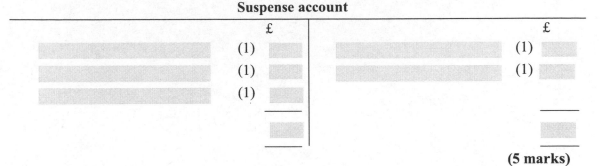

(5 marks)

(b)   Complete the following sales ledger control account to reconcile the difference
between the balance on the sales ledger control account in the original trial balance
and the sum of the individual customer balances in the sales ledger. The original
control account balance was £327,762.

Assuming that after correction of the sales ledger control account this reconciles with
the sales ledger listing total, what is the sales ledger listing total?

*Marks are awarded for completing the gaps where a mark (in brackets) is indicated.
There are no marks for completing the missing words or figures where no mark is
indicated but these will help you to obtain the correct answers.*

Sales ledger control account

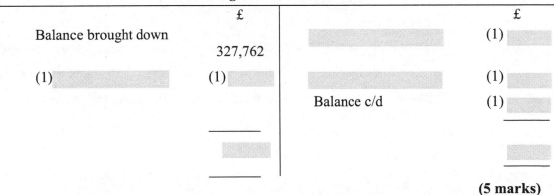

(5 marks)

(c)   Complete the following statement of adjusted net profit showing both the original net profit of £412,967 as given by the draft accounts and the net profit after correcting items (1) to (7) above.

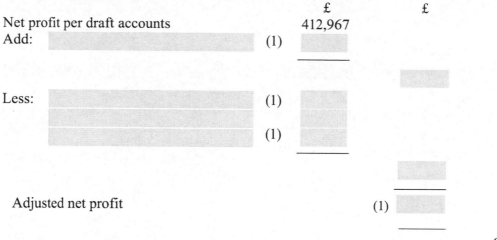

	£	£
Net profit per draft accounts	412,967	
Add: _____ (1)	_____	
		_____
Less: _____ (1)	_____	
_____ (1)		
	_____	
		_____
Adjusted net profit (1)		_____
		_____

(5 marks)

11   TD

At the year end of TD, an imbalance in the trial balance was revealed which resulted in the creation of a suspense account with a credit balance of £1,040.

Investigations revealed the following errors:

(i)   A sale of goods on credit for £1,000 had been omitted from the sales account.

(ii)   Delivery and installation costs of £240 on a new item of plant had been recorded as a revenue expense.

(iii) Cash discount of £150 on paying a creditor, JW, had been taken, even though the payment was made outside the time limit.

(iv)   Stock of stationery at the end of the period of £240 had been ignored.

(v)   A purchase of raw materials of £350 had been recorded in the purchases account as £850.

(vi)   The purchase returns day book included a sales credit note for £230 which had been entered correctly in the account of the debtor concerned, but included with purchase returns in the nominal ledger.

Required:

(a)   Complete the missing words and figures in the following journal entries to correct EACH of the above errors. Narratives are NOT required.

Marks are awarded for completing the gaps where a mark (in brackets) is indicated. There are no marks for completing the missing words or figures where no mark is indicated but these will help you to obtain the correct answers.

TD – Journal entries

		Debit £	Credit £
(i)	Suspense account (1)		
	(1)		
(ii)	Plant at cost		
	(1)		
(iii)	Discounts (1)		
	(1)		
(iv)	Stationery (1)		
	Stationery (1)		
(v)	Suspense account	500	
	(1) (1)		
(vi)	(1)		
	(1)		
	Suspense account		460

(12 marks)

(b) Complete the following suspense account and show the corrections to be made.

Marks are awarded for completing the gaps where a mark (in brackets) is indicated. There are no marks for completing the missing words or figures where no mark is indicated but these will help you to obtain the correct answers.

Suspense account

	£		£
(1)		Balance per trial balance	1,040
(1)		(1)	

(3 marks)

(c) Prior to the discovery of the errors, TD's gross profit for the year was calculated at £35,750 and the net profit for the year at £18,500.

Calculate the revised gross and net profit figures after the correction of the errors.

Marks are awarded for completing the gaps where a mark (in brackets) is indicated. There are no marks for completing the missing words or figures where no mark is indicated but these will help you to obtain the correct answers.

		£
Gross profit – original		35,750
Revised gross profit	(2)	
Net profit – original		18,500
Revised net profit	(3)	

(5 marks)

12   MMM LTD

MMM Ltd is a recently formed company which provides training and educational services. The company was formed with an authorised share capital of 1,000,000 £1 shares. The three shareholders, who are also directors, each purchased 120,000 shares at £1.40 per share. It is expected that the business will grow rapidly during the first two years, and that funds for that expansion will be sought by issuing shares to family members and obtaining bank finance.

During the first year of trading, a net profit (before tax) of £48,800 was made, after deducting salaries to the three directors of £60,000 in total. Corporation tax of £6,500 was provided for the year. As well as the salaries, the three directors declared dividends for themselves of 5p per share. They also decided to transfer £5,000 into general reserves.

During the second year of trading, net profit (before tax) was £55,000. Family members purchased a further 30,000 shares at £1.50 per share, at the start of the year. Salaries were as in the first year. Dividends of 8p per share were paid. Corporation tax of £8,000 was provided for the year, and a further £5,000 transferred into general reserves.

Required:

Complete the missing words and figures in the following:

(a)   The appropriation accounts for each of years 1 and 2.

Marks are awarded for completing the gaps where a mark (in brackets) is indicated. There are no marks for completing the missing words or figures where no mark is indicated but these will help you obtain the correct answers.

MMM Ltd - Profit and loss appropriation accounts

		£	£
		Year 1	Year 2
Profit before tax		48,800	55,000
Corporation tax		(6,500)	(8,000)
Profit after tax		42,300	47,000
Dividends	(1)		(1)
Transfer to reserves	(1)		(1)
Retained profit			

(4 marks)

(b) The capital section of the balance sheet for each of years 1 and 2.

Marks are awarded for completing the gaps where a mark (in brackets) is indicated. There are no marks for completing the missing words or figures where no mark is indicated but these will help you obtain the correct answers.

MMM Ltd - Capital and reserves

		£		£
		Year 1		Year 2
Issued share capital	(1)		(1)	
Share premium	(1)		(1)	
General reserve	(1)		(1)	
P & L account	(1)		(1)	

(8 marks)

(c) Tick all boxes that apply to the following statements.

	True	False
The purpose of the internal audit is to provide an independent check on the stewardship function of the directors.	☐	☐
The external auditor reports to the directors of the company.	☐	☐
The auditor checks that the company has a proper system of accounting records that is adequate to produce a true and fair set of financial statements.	☐	☐
The auditor will also attempt to discover any fraudulent activities which is a primary purpose of an audit.	☐	☐

(4 marks)

ACCRUALS, PREPAYMENTS, STOCKS, DEBTORS AND FIXED ASSETS

13 JOHN BARKER

John Barker's business has a year end of 31 December 20X8 and he is now considering the accruals and prepayments for that year.

Required:

(a)   What does the accruals concept state?

(*Your answer must not exceed 20 words.*)

(2 marks)

(b)   (i)   John Barker paid telephone charges of £1,000 for 1 January 20X8 to 30 November 20X8 and £300 for the quarter ended February 20X9. How much should he charge in the year ended 31 December 20X8?

£

(2 marks)

(ii)   He also paid insurance annually in advance on 1 April. The premium to 31 March 20X8 was £4,000 and to 31 March 20X9 was £4,800. How much should he charge at 31 December 20X8?

£

(2 marks)

(c)   Tick all boxes that apply.

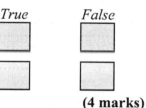

	True	False
Accruals and prepayments never apply to items of miscellaneous income.		
Accruals and prepayments are short-term in nature.		

(4 marks)

14 PROVISION

The balance on the provision for doubtful debts account on 1 January 20X1 was £1,000, equal to 5% of debtors at that date.

In the 12 months to 31 December 20X1 sales are £90,000, cash receipts from sales are £80,000 and bad debts (charged to the provision account) are £600. The doubtful debts provision balance at close of business on 31 December 20X1 is required to be 5% of debtors.

In the 12 months to 31 December 20X2 sales are £100,000, cash receipts from sales are £110,000 and bad debts (charged directly to expenses) are £400. The doubtful debts provision balance at close of business on 31 December 20X2 is required to be 5% of debtors. (The change in treatment of bad debts in the second year does not imply that an adjustment or correction should be made in relation to the first year.)

Required:

(a)   Complete the following provision for doubtful debts account for the period 1 January 20X1 to 1 January 20X3, clearly bringing down the balance at the end of each year, and indicating the double entry for each item in the account.

Marks are awarded for completing the gaps where a mark (in brackets) is indicated. There are no marks for completing the missing words or figures where no mark is indicated but these will help you to obtain the correct answers.

Provision for doubtful debts

20X1			£	20X1			£
31.12	(1)		(1)	1.1	(1)		
31.12	Balance c/f		(1)	31.12	P & L a/c		(1)
20X2				20X2			
31.12	P & L a/c		(1)	1.1	Balance brought forward		
31.12	Balance c/f		(1)				

(7 marks)

(b) Is the balance on the provision for doubtful debts account a liability? Explain your answer briefly but clearly in less than 30 words.

(5 marks)

15 COST AND NRV

'The idea that stock should be included in accounts at the lower of historical cost and net realisable value follows the prudence convention but not the consistency convention.'

Required:

(a) Explain clearly what is meant by the following terms.

(Your answer for each explanation should not exceed 20 words.)

(i)	Historical cost	**(1 mark)**
(ii)	Net realisable value	**(2 marks)**
(iii)	Prudence convention	**(2 marks)**
(iv)	Consistency convention	**(2 marks)**

(b) Do you agree with the quotation? **(4 marks)**

(c) Explain, with reasons, whether you think this idea (that stocks should be included in accounts at the lower of historical cost and net realisable value) is a useful one. Refer to at least two classes of user of financial accounting reports in your answer.

(6 marks)

16 JAY LTD

Jay Ltd values stocks on the First In First Out (FIFO) basis. During October 20X9, there are the following details regarding stocks of product A:

1 October	Balance in stock	120 items valued at £8 each
3 October	Purchases	180 items at £9 each
4 October	Sales	150 items at £12 each
8 October	Sales	80 items at £15 each

12 October	Returns to the supplier	30 items purchased on 3 October
18 October	Purchases	300 items at £10 each
22 October	Sales	100 items at £15 each
28 October	Returns from customers	20 items sold on 22 October

Required:

(a) Complete the following stores ledger card for product A for October 20X9 using the FIFO method.

Note: Goods returned in are valued at the latest issue price.

Marks are awarded for completing the gaps where a mark (in brackets) is indicated. There are no marks for completing the missing words or figures where no mark is included but these will help you to obtain the correct answers.

	Receipts			Issues			Balance	
Date	Quantity	Price £	Value £	Quantity	Price £	Value £	Quantity	Value £
October								
1	120	8	▓				120	▓
3	180	9	▓				300	▓
4				▓	▓	▓		
				(1)▓	▓	▓		
				150		▓	▓	▓
8				▓	▓	▓	▓	▓
12				▓	▓	▓	▓	▓
18	300	10	3,000				340	(1)▓
22				▓	▓	▓		
				▓	▓	▓		
				▓		▓	(1)▓	▓
28	20	10	200				(1)▓	▓

(4 marks)

(b) Complete the following stores ledger card for product A for October 20X9 using the AVCO (Weighted Average Cost) method. (Prices are to be calculated to one decimal place).

Marks are awarded for completing the gaps where a mark (in brackets) is indicated. There are no marks for completing the missing words or figures where no mark is included but these will help you to obtain the correct answers.

Date	Receipts			Issues			Balance	
	Quantity	Price £	Value £	Quantity	Price £	Value £	Quantity	Value £
October								
1	120	8	960				120	960
3	180	9	1,620				300	2,580
4					(1)			
8								
12					(1)			
18	300	10	3,000					
22					(1)			
28								(1)

(4 marks)

(c) The gross profit for October using:

    (i)   the FIFO method is £ ⬜

    (ii)   the AVCO method is £ ⬜   **(4 marks)**

(d) Complete the missing words below:

    (i)   The financial statements of most companies are prepared on the basis of the ⬜ cost convention.   **(2 marks)**

    (ii)   In the balance sheet the stocks of the business must be shown at the lower of ⬜ value.   **(2 marks)**

FINANCIAL STATEMENTS AND RATIO ANALYSIS

17 OWNER OF A BUSINESS

The owner of a business may choose to run it as a sole trader or as a limited liability company. The following is a list of differences between the two methods of operation. Complete the blanks in the differences using the following list of words/phrases.

List of words/phrases

    separate legal entities
    exempt
    Memorandum and articles of association
    sole trader
    business itself
    limited to
    directors
    shares rather than the business itself
    Companies Acts
    shareholders
    shareholders
    profit of the business

dividends out of the profits of the business
separate
unlimited liability

Differences between the two methods of operation

	Sole trader	Limited company	
Legal entity	The business is not ▓▓▓▓ from the owner	Companies are ▓▓▓▓ in law – they can sue and be sued.	(2 marks)
Ownership	The business is owned by the ▓▓▓▓	The company is owned by ▓▓▓▓	(2 marks)
Legal control	Little statutory control.	Companies must comply with company rules being governed by the ▓▓▓▓	(1 mark)
Liability	Sole trader has ▓▓▓▓ ▓▓▓▓ to creditors.	The liability of shareholders is ▓▓▓▓ the capital already introduced by them.	(2 marks)
Constitution	No formal constitution required.	The objects, powers and duties of a company must be set out in its ▓▓▓▓ ▓▓▓▓	(1 mark)
Audit	An audit is not required.	An audit is required (unless ▓▓▓▓ as a small company) which is a substantial cost.	(1 mark)
Management	By the owner.	Separation of management (by ▓▓▓▓) from ownership (by the ▓▓▓▓).	(2 marks)
Returns	The owner takes all the ▓▓▓▓ .	The owners (shareholders) may receive ▓▓▓▓ .	(2 marks)
Transfer of ownership	By transfer of the ▓▓▓▓ .	By transfer of the ▓▓▓▓ .	(2 marks)

18   CASH FLOW STATEMENT

A cash flow statement shows the effect of a company's commercial transactions on its cash balance. Profit does not equal cash.

(a)   Complete the missing words in the following statement explaining the purpose of cash flow statements. (½ mark per word/phrase.)

The purpose of a cash flow statement is to provide additional information to the ▓▓▓▓ account and the ▓▓▓▓ . The cash flow statement shows the reasons for the change in the ▓▓▓▓ balances over the accounting period. ▓▓▓▓ is vital to an organisation so the information that the cash flow statement provides is of great use to ▓▓▓▓ of the accounts as it is different to the information provided in the ▓▓▓▓ .   (3 marks)

(b) Complete the missing words in the following statement explaining the use of cash flow statements. (½ mark per word/phrase.)

The main use of the cash flow statement is in analysing the __________ . It shows the ability of the organisation to generate cash from __________ and then shows how that cash has been __________ over the period. It shows how finance has been serviced in the form of __________ paid and __________ paid. It shows monies spent on and received from the sale of __________ assets. It also shows receipts and payments for loans and __________ . **(3 marks)**

(c) Define the following terms in a cash flow statement:

(i) Liquid resources **(2 marks)**

(ii) Net debt **(2 marks)**

(Your answer for each definition must not exceed 20 words.)

(d) Tick the boxes that apply:

	True	*False*
(i) The two methods of completing the reconciliation of operating profit to net cash inflow from operating activities are the direct and indirect methods.	☐	☐
(ii) Operating profit for cash flow statement is the profit figure **after** interest and tax.	☐	☐
(iii) In the movements in working capital items:		
- an increase in stock means you paid out more cash.	☐	☐
- an increase in debtors means you received less cash.	☐	☐
- an increase in creditors means you paid more cash.	☐	☐

(10 marks)

19   BETA

Beta Limited is reviewing the financial statements of two companies, Zeta Limited and Omega Limited.

The companies trade as wholesalers, selling electrical goods to retailers on credit.

Their most recent financial statements appear below.

	Zeta Limited		Omega Limited	
	£000	£000	£000	£000
Fixed assets				
Tangible assets				
Warehouse and office buildings	1,200		5,000	
Equipment and vehicles	600		1,000	
	———		———	
Current assets		1,800		6,000
Stock	400		800	
Trade debtors	800		900	
Sundry debtors	150		80	
Cash at bank	-		100	
	———		———	
	1,350		1,880	
	———		———	
Current liabilities				
Trade creditors	800		800	
Sundry creditors	80		100	
Overdraft	200		-	
Taxation	120		90	
	———		———	
	1,200		990	
	———		———	
Net current assets		150		890
		———		———
		1,950		6,890
Long-term loan (interest 10% per annum)		-		(4,000)
		———		———
		1,950		2,890
		———		———
Capital and reserves				
Share capital		1,000		1,600
Revaluation reserve		-		500
Profit and loss account		950		790
		———		———
		1,950		2,890
		———		———

Profit and loss accounts for the year ended 31 March 20X8

	Zeta Limited		Omega Limited	
	£000	£000	£000	£000
Sales		4,000		6,000
Cost of sales				
Opening stock	200		800	
Purchases	3,200		4,800	
	3,400		5,600	
Less closing stock	400		800	
		3,000		4,800
Gross profit		1,000		1,200
Expenses				
Distribution costs	200		150	
Administrative expenses	290		250	
Interest paid	10		400	
		500		800
Profit before tax		500		400
Taxation		120		90
Net profit for the period		380		310

Required:

(a)   Complete the missing figures in the following list of ratios. (1 mark per ratio).

Marks are awarded for completing the gaps where a mark (in brackets) is indicated. There are no marks for completing the missing words or figures where no mark is indicated but these will help you obtain the correct answers.

	Zeta Ltd	Omega Ltd
Profitability		
Return on capital employed		

Return on owners' equity

Gross profit margin

Omega Ltd:

$$\frac{1,200}{6,000}$$

$$= 20\%$$

Net operating profit margin

$=$

Liquidity

Current ratio

$=$

Quick ratio

$=$

Working capital management

Stock turnover $\times 365$ $\times 365$

$=$ days $=$ days

Debtor days $\times 365$ $\times 365$

$=$ days $=$ days

Creditor days $\times 365$ $\times 365$

$=$ days $=$ days

(9 marks)

(b) Tick the boxes that apply to the following statements (1 mark for each tick).

	True	*False*

(i) *Profitability*

	True	False
Zeta has a considerably higher return on capital employed and return on owners' equity than Omega. A contributing factor could be the revaluation of Omega's fixed assets. This would immediately increase capital employed, but would not affect profit. This in turn reduces the return.	☐	☐
Zeta has a slightly lower gross profit margin than Omega, which suggests differences in pricing structures.	☐	☐
When interest is excluded, Zeta Ltd shows a lower fall in gross profit to operating profit owing to its higher expense figures.	☐	☐

(ii)   *Liquidity*

	True	False
Here Omega shows the better position partly because Zeta has an overdraft and no cash balance.	☐	☐
However, Omega has a much lower stock figure. Depending on the reason, this could actually distort the current ratio to give a gloomier picture.	☐	☐

(iii)   *Working capital management*

	True	False
Omega has better credit control for its debtors but it not as successful at turning over stock. Omega may also consider lengthening creditors' payment period to be consistent with the industry average.	☐	☐
Zeta has a more efficient stock turnover rate but its debtor and creditor management reinforces its liquidity problem.	☐	☐
Both companies are at least paying their creditors after collecting cash from debtors.	☐	☐
High gearing suggests a low financial risk.	☐	☐
An increase in trade would have more of an impact for Zeta by increasing the margin between the financing interest rate and Zeta's return.	☐	☐

(10 marks)

20   ARH PLC

ARH plc has the following results for the last two years of trading:

ARH plc – Trading and profit and loss account

for the year ended	31.12.X4	31.12.X5
	£000	£000
Sales	14,400	17,000
Less: Cost of sales	11,800	12,600
Gross profit	2,600	4,400
Less: Expenses	1,200	2,000
Net profit for the year	1,400	2,400
Dividends	520	780
Retained profit for the year	880	1,620

ARH plc – Balance sheet at	31 December 20X4		31 December 20X5	
	£000	£000	£000	£000
Fixed assets		2,500		4,000
Current assets:				
Stocks	1,300		2,000	
Debtors	2,000		1,600	
Bank balances	2,400		820	
	5,700		4,420	
Less: Current liabilities:				
Creditors	1,500		2,700	
		4,200		1,720
		6,700		5,720
Less: Long-term liabilities:				
10% debentures		2,600		-
		4,100		5,720
Financed by:				
2.4 million ordinary shares of £1 each		2,400		2,400
Revaluation reserve		500		500
Retained profits		1,200		2,820
		4,100		5,720

Required:

(a)   Complete the missing words and figures in the following calculations and comments on accounting ratios.

Marks are awarded for completing the gaps where a mark (in brackets) is indicated. There are no marks for completing the missing words or figures where no mark is indicated but these will help you obtain the correct answers.

	20X4	20X5
Gross profit ratio		
$\dfrac{\text{Gross profit}}{\text{Sales}} \times 100$	$\times 100$	$\times 100$
	= (1) %	= (1) %
Net profit ratio		
$\dfrac{\text{Net profit}}{\text{Sales}} \times 100$	$\times 100$	$\times 100$
	= (1) %	= (1) %
Return on capital employed		
$\dfrac{\text{Net profit}}{} \times 100$	$\times 100$	$\times 100$
	= (1) %	= (1) %
Average total capital		
	=	=

In 20X5 ARH has managed to increase its turnover by (1)   % as well as increasing gross margin and net margin. It is not known whether the increase in turnover is just to do with the increased margins or whether there has been an actual increase in (1)   of sales.

Return on capital employed has also increased and this is due partly to an increased profitability and also partly due to decreased (1) ⬚ .

	20X4	20X5
Current ratio	⬚	⬚
	(1) ⬚	(1) ⬚
Acid test ratio	⬚	⬚
	(1) ⬚	(1) ⬚

One of the major reasons for the decrease in cash is due to the changes in the (1) ⬚ of ARH. The loan of £2.6 million has been paid off over the period and obviously this has had a major impact on the cash balances of the business.

In conclusion the position of ARH has gone from a very healthy cash position which might even be seen as over cautious to what might be seen as a slightly risky position.

(14 marks)

(b)   Explain what is meant by the accounting term *reserves*.

(Your answer must not exceed 20 words.)

(2 marks)

(c)   Explain how the item 'revaluation reserve' in the above balance sheets might have arisen.

(Your answer must not exceed 20 words.)

(2 marks)

Section 3

ANSWERS TO OBJECTIVE TEST QUESTIONS

CONCEPTUAL AND REGULATORY FRAMEWORK

1   B

The other answers are also aims of accounting, but are subsidiary to the main aim of providing financial information.

2   C

Financial accounts are normally published annually, to provide information to external users (e.g. shareholders). Both financial accounts and management accounts contain details of various costs that form part of the trial balance, so answer D is not correct.

3   D

If a business is a going concern, it is reasonable to assume that fixed assets will be used over their expected useful economic life. It is therefore appropriate to value a fixed asset at cost less accumulated depreciation, which represents the consumption of value so far.

4   C

If the net realisable value (NRV) of stock is less than its cost, it is prudent to write down the stock from cost to NRV. The amount written off is recorded as a loss. The loss is taken 'now' (as soon as it is recognised), rather than at a later time, when it is sold.

5   D

If there is no new capital introduced in the period, retained profit can be measured as the rise in the value of net assets between the beginning and the end of the period. (Profit would be retained profit + drawings/dividends in the period.)

6   B

The historical cost concept is to value assets and liabilities at their original cost to the business, and so fails to take account of changing price levels over time. This is a particular problem with assets that are held for a long time and tend to rise in value, particularly land and buildings. However, the historical cost concept does have regard to depreciation of fixed assets and loss in value, so answer C is incorrect.

7   C

A definition of 'true and fair view' often includes a reference to the financial statements being prepared in accordance with generally accepted accounting practice.

8   D

Profits are overstated, in the sense that the cost of sales and expenses are measured at their historical cost, not at their current value at the time of sale or consumption. Balance sheet values are understated, because they are recorded at cost rather than at their current value.

9   C

Accounting standards in the UK are issued by the Accounting Standards Board (ASB).

10   D

There is no legal or regulatory requirement to adjust asset values, nor limit dividend payments, in a period of inflation.

11   B

Capital maintenance is the concept that profit can only be earned after a sufficient allowance has been provided in costs to maintain the capital of the business, in financial terms or in terms of physical/operating capability.

12   B

Profit is the increase in net assets between the beginning and end of the period, plus drawings taken out of the business, minus new capital introduced in the period (which is not profit).

13   B

Purchases should be recorded when the transaction takes place, which in this case is on receipt of the stock. If a business waits until receipt of the invoice to record a purchase, there could be an opportunity for 'window dressing' of the accounts at the end of the year, by asking suppliers not to send in invoices until later.

14   A

Consistency means using the same accounting policies from one year to the next. Asset valuations and profit measurements are made the same way each year, and this makes it easier to compare the financial position and performance of the business between one year and the next.

15   D

Falling prices (deflation) are not usual. If deflation does occur, historical cost accounting will overstate the current value of assets in the balance sheet. Profits will be understated. Perhaps the easiest way to think about this is that if fixed assets are valued at historical cost when their current value is much lower due to deflation, depreciation charges will be higher and profit lower.

16   C

Statement C is incorrect. The difference between financial accounting and management accounting has nothing to do with accuracy.

17   C

The responsibility for ensuring the company maintains proper accounting records rests with the directors of the company.

18   D

Capital expenditure is expenditure on the acquisition or improvement of long-term (fixed) assets for a business. Repairs and maintenance costs are 'revenue expenditure' and chargeable against profit in the period they are incurred. An issue of share capital involves receiving new capital, not spending it.

19   A

Safeguarding and making proper use of the assets of a business is a function of 'stewardship', which is the responsibility of a company's directors.

20   D

Painting and replacing windows are maintenance and repairs, and so are classified as 'revenue expenditure'. The purchase of a car for re-sale means that the car is an item of stock for the business, not a fixed asset. Legal fees incurred in purchasing a building are included in the cost of the building, and so are part of the fixed asset cost, i.e. capital expenditure.

21   C

Assets – Liabilities – Opening capital + Drawings = Profit

22   D

Stock costing £400 is sold for £1,000, giving a profit of £600. The VAT on the sale will be £175.

	Cash £	Stock £	Liabilities £	Capital £
Start business	1,000			1,000
Buy stock		800	800	
Sell stock	1,175	(400)	175	600
	2,175	400	975	1,600

23   B

	£
Closing capital	4,500
Opening capital	(10,000)
Decrease in net assets	(5,500)
Drawings: profit taken out	8,000
Capital introduced	(4,000)
Loss for the year	(1,500)

24   C

Stewardship means 'looking after', and this function is best described by answer C.

ACCOUNTING SYSTEMS

25   £7,700

The contra transaction should have been recorded as:

Debit:	Purchase ledger control account (creditors)	£400
Credit:	Sales ledger control account (debtors)	£400.

However, by debiting the sales ledger control account, instead of crediting it, total debtors have been over-stated by 2 × £400 (£800), and should be £7,700 rather than £8,500.

26   £3,770

The balance sheet figure is the original cash book balance adjusted for items in the bank statement that need to be recorded in the cash book.

27   £3,170

	£
Overdraft in cash book	(4,360)
Items in bank statement but not in cash book:	
Bank charges	(120)
Bank overdraft interest	(90)
Credit transfer into the account	2,500
Direct debit payment	(1,700)
Adjusted cash book: *balance sheet figure*	(3,770)
Items in cash book but not bank statement:	
Payments received	(3,600)
Payments to suppliers	4,200
Bank statement balance	(3,170)

28   B

The journal, petty cash book and sales day book are all books of prime entry. The petty cash book (like the cash book) is also an account in the double entry system (the main/general/nominal ledger). The purchase ledger is neither a day book nor a part of the double entry system.

29   £603

Creditors account

	£		£
Bank	1,470	Balance b/d	540
Purchase returns	33	Purchasés (on credit)	1,590
Discounts received	24		
Balance c/d	603		
	2,130		2,130
		Balance b/d	603

30   D

VAT account

	£		£
Creditors/bank	6,000	Balance b/d	3,400
Bank	2,600	Debtors/bank	10,500
Balance c/d	5,300		
	13,900		13,900
		Balance b/d	5,300

VAT on sales (outputs) = 17.5% × £60,000 = £10,500.

VAT on purchases (inputs) = (17.5/117.5) × £40,286 = £6,000

31   B

VAT is chargeable on the price after deducting the bulk purchase discount of 20%. The full purchase price is therefore 1.175 × £1,600 = £1,880. Since the trader is not registered for VAT, the purchases account should be debited with this full amount, including the tax. (A different situation arises when a trader is registered for VAT.)

32   D

The purchase day book has been undercast by £500 (i.e. the total is £500 lower than it should be). As a result of this, the purchases account has been debited and the purchase ledger control account (total creditors) credited with £500 too little.

The sales day book has been overcast by £700. As a result, the sales account has been credited and the sales ledger control account (total debtors) has been debited with £700 too much.

As a result of these errors, the control account balances need to be adjusted, and profit reduced by (£500 + £700) £1,200, by reducing sales and increasing purchases.

Neither error affects the entries in the accounts of individual debtors and creditors.

33   B

The total charge for wages is the gross wages of employees, plus the employer's national insurance contributions. Here, the total is £157,326 + £33,247 = £190,573.

34   £4,009

A debit balance on the creditors' ledger means that the business is owed money by its creditors, perhaps for sales returns or because of an overpayment. Here the debit balances are being transferred to the debtors' ledger, and the accounting entry to record this is: Credit Creditors, Debit Debtors.

Creditors account

	£		£
Bank	271,845	Balance b/d	76,104
Discounts received	5,698	Purchases	286,932
Contra: debtors ledger	866	Debtors ledger	107
Balances written off	82		
Purchase returns (balancing figure)	4,009		
Balance c/d	80,643		
	363,143		363,143
		Balance b/d	80,643

35   A

As a result of the error, total creditors are under-stated by £259,440 - £254,940 = £4,500. To correct the error, we need to increase the balance in the creditors' ledger control account, and this is done by crediting the control account.

The error has affected the control account only, and not the entries in the individual creditor account for Figgins in the purchase ledger, so the total of creditors' balances is unaffected.

36   B

You think that you owe £150 more than the supplier has stated. With items, A, C and D the result would be that the supplier will state that you owe more, not less, than you think.

37   B

A straightforward question compared with many others! Sales are recorded at their value excluding VAT, as credit items (income).

38   B

Debit balances represent assets or expenses (and drawings).

Credit balances represent liabilities, capital or income.

Carriage outwards is an expense and a prepayment is an asset.

39   D

Credit balances represent liabilities, capital or income, and the question is arguably incorrect to omit 'capital'. However, item D is the only possible answer.

40   C

This is another straightforward double entry question. The car is an asset (debit), capital is a credit.

41   B

The debtors account should be debited with the full amount payable, including the tax. The entry in the sales account should be for the sales value excluding VAT. VAT payable to the tax authorities should be credited to the VAT account (liability = credit balance).

42   A

The debtors account should be credited with the full amount of the sales return, including the tax. The Sales returns account should be debited with the value of the returns excluding the VAT. The VAT account should be debited with the amount of tax on the returns (since the tax is no longer payable).

43   D

The sales day book provides totals for debtors, sales excluding VAT and VAT on the sales. These totals are transferred to the nominal ledger by debiting total debtors account with the gross amount payable, crediting the sales account with the value of sales excluding VAT and crediting VAT account with the amount of VAT payable.

44   D

Items A and B will result in an error in the control account (total debtors). Item C will result in an error in the total of individual debtor account balances. Item D will not affect either of the totals, although there are errors in the individual accounts of the two customers affected, with one account balance too high and the other too low by the same amount.

45   A

The series of transactions might be recorded as follows.

Original purchase

   Debit Purchases

   Credit Brad (creditor)

On payment

   Debit Brad (creditor)

   Credit Bank

On cancellation of the cheque

   Debit Bank

   Credit Returns outwards

If the second and third transactions are dealt with at the same time, they simplify to Debit Brad, credit Returns outwards.

46   £390

	£
Bank statement balance	(825)
Item not yet recorded in cash book	
Bank charges	(50)
Error in bank records	
Add direct debit incorrectly charged	160
Items in cash book but not yet in bank statement	
Unpresented cheques	(475)
Deposits not yet recorded	800
Balance in cash book (for balance sheet)	(390)

47   B

When you pay a creditor too much, the creditor will owe money to you, and so is a debtor. This would explain a debit balance on a creditor account.

48   B

It is easy to get confused about credits and debits with a bank account. In the accounts of a business, cash is shown as a debit balance and an overdraft is a credit balance. Cash paid into the account is debited and cash paid out is credited to the Bank account. To a bank, however, money in a customer's account is money that the bank owes to the customer, and to the bank, this is a credit item. This is why a bank might 'credit your account' by putting money into it. This meaning of crediting an account is used in this question.

	£
Cash book balance	(8,970)
Items on bank statement, but not in cash book	
Bank charges	(550)
Bank error	425
Items not yet on the bank statement	
Payments from the account	3,275
Receipts into the account	(5,380)
Bank statement balance	(11,200)

49 £1,970

	£
Balance at start of month	2,500
Payment (£800 less 10%)	(720)
Receipt (£200 less 5%)	190
Balance at end of month	1,970

50 A

Purchase ledger control account

	£		£
Bank	68,900	Opening balance b/d	34,500
Discounts received	1,200	Purchases (credit)	78,400
Purchase returns	4,700		
Closing balance c/d	38,100		
	112,900		112,900
		Opening balance b/d	38,100

51 B

	£
Bank statement balance	13,400
Items not recorded in the cash book	
Dishonoured cheque	300
Bank charges	50
	13,750
Unpresented cheques	(1,400)
Error: receipt recorded as a payment (2 × £195)	(390)
Cash book balance before corrections	11,960

52 D

£14.10 + £25.50 + £12.90 + (£24.00 × 1.175) = £80.70.

53 C

It might not be easy to identify the correct solution to this question. A trial balance does not confirm the accuracy of the ledger accounts, nor does it provide information for calculating adjustments. Neither does it provide all the figures necessary to prepare the final accounts, even though it provides many of them. For example, the trial balance does not include a closing stock figure. Almost by default, answer C is the correct answer.

54   **£15,000**

Sales ledger control account

	£		£
Opening balance b/d	14,500	Discounts allowed	350
Sales	53,500	Contra: purchase ledger	50
		Sales returns	1,400
		Bank	51,200
		Balance c/d	15,000
	68,000		68,000
Balance b/d	15,000		

55   **D**

The balance on the control account exceeds the total of the individual account balances by £1,802. Items A, B and C would all have the effect of making the total of the individual account balances higher by £1,802. Item D, however, by recording a credit item as a debit item in the control account, has made the control account debit balance too high by £901 × 2 = £1,802.

56   **D**

All these codes might be used in a computerised accounting system.

57   **B**

Presumably, there was no opening balance on this account.

Sales ledger control account

	£		£
Sales	250,000	Bank	225,000
Bank: cheque returned	3,500	Sales returns	2,500
		Bad debts	3,000
		Contra: purchase ledger	4,000
		Balance c/d	19,000
	253,500		253,500
Balance b/d	19,000		

58   **D**

In an imprest system, petty cash is periodically topped up to a specific maximum limit. The amount of new cash added to petty cash should equal the sum of the expenditures on all the petty cash vouchers created since the previous top-up.

59   **A**

The total cost of salaries charged to the profit and loss account is the total gross salaries plus employers' national insurance contributions.

60   **D**

Day books are records of prime entry, i.e. used to make the first record of a transaction in the accounting system.

61   C

The creditor is owed the full amount of the invoice, including the VAT, so the credit entry in the supplier account must be $9,200. The fixed asset account is recorded at cost excluding the VAT. The input VAT is recoverable, so debit the VAT account with $1,200.

62   C

	$
Net pay in February	1,540
Tax for January	500
National Insurance for January	100
	2,140

63   B

A debit balance on a purchase ledger account means that the business is owed money by its supplier. This could be explained by the company mistakenly paying too much. (For example, a business might pay the full amount of an invoice and then receive a 'credit note' from the supplier for the return of faulty goods.)

64   D

	£
April net salaries	14,000
April tax and employees' National Insurance	6,000
April employer's National Insurance	1,500
	21,500

The profit and loss account shows the expenses which relate to the period, irrespective of when they were paid.

65   D

	£
Gross salary	1,000
Employer's National Insurance	100
	1,100

66   D

VAT should still be accounted for by a VAT-registered business, irrespective of whether the customer is VAT registered or not. For example, a retailer charges consumers VAT, and consumers are not VAT-registered.

67   C

The control account cannot ensure that the personal ledger is free from error. The two totals can agree, but there may be compensating errors in the personal ledger (e.g. the wrong account is debited) or an entry may be missing from both the control account and the ledger.

68   A

	£
Balance per bank statement 31 December 20X7	21,720
Less: Outstanding cheques	2,500
	19,220

69   D

	£
Balance per bank statement	(715)
Add: Unpresented cheques	(824)
	(1,539)
Less: Outstanding lodgements	337
	(1,202)
Add: Bank error	(25)
Balance sheet/cash book overdraft	(1,227)

70   D

	£
Current bank balance	(5,675)
Standing order entered twice	125
	(5,550)
Dishonoured cheque (2 × £450)	(900)
	(6,450)

Note: The dishonoured cheque for £450 should have been credited to the bank balance. Instead it was debited. The bank balance is therefore too high by £900.

71   B

Debtors' ledger control account

	£		£
Balance b/f	10,000	Receipts	90,000
Sales	100,000	Discounts allowed	800
Debt reinstated	1,000	Balance c/f	20,200
	111,000		111,000

72   B

Cash book

	£		£
Cash sales	1,450	Balance b/f	485
Cash receipts	2,400	Payments to creditors (95% × £1,800)	1,710
		Reinstate debtors for dishonoured cheques	250
		Balance c/f (balancing figure)	1,405
	3,850		3,850
Balance b/f	1,405		

73   D

Total creditors

	£		£
Cash paid	542,300	Opening creditors	142,600
Discounts received	13,200		
Goods returned	27,500		
Closing creditors	137,800	Purchases	578,200
	720,800		720,800

74   C

Debtors control account

	£		£
Balance brought forward	10,000	Receipts from credit sales	80,000
Sales on credit			
(balancing figure)	79,000	Balance c/f	9,000
	89,000		89,000

75   C

'Prime' means first, and a book of prime entry is where accounting transactions are recorded in the first instance within the accounting system. From the books of prime entry, transactions are subsequently transferred to the ledger accounts.

76   C

This is an important rule to know. Asset balances and expenses are debit balances in the nominal ledger accounts, and liabilities, income and capital are all credit balances.

77   B

The balance per the bank statement needs to be adjusted for the unpresented cheque (£800 + £80 = £880). The dishonoured cheque must also be entered in the cash book, but the bank statement balance already allows for this.

78   D

A credit entry in the accounts of Y means either that Y owes X £450 or that X owes Y £450 less than before. A credit entry would arise in Y's debtors ledger if customer X returned goods to Y. All the other transactions in the question would result in debit entries.

79   B

	£	£
Balance per cash book		2,490
Less: bank charges not in cash book	50	
dishonoured cheque	140	
		(190)
Corrected cash book balance		2,300

80   C

	£
Opening capital	6,500
Profit for the year less drawings	32,500
VAT adjustment to telephone bill (£400 × 17.5%)	(70)
Closing capital	38,930

81   D

Charged to profit and loss account:	£
Basic pay (36 hours × £3.50)	126.00
Employer's national insurance (10% × £126)	12.60
	138.60

Paid to employee:	£
Basic pay (as above)	126.00
Less:	
Tax (20% × (£126 – £75))	(10.20)
Employee's NI (7% × £126)	(8.82)
	106.98

82   A

	£
Balance per cash book	(1,240)
Unpresented cheques	450
Unrecorded receipt	(140)
Bank charges	(75)
Balance per bank statement	(1,005)

83   D

	£
Net wages paid	240,500
Add:	
Contributions to pension scheme	12,500
Employees' tax and National Insurance	64,000
Employees' gross wages	317,000
Employer's National Insurance	22,000
	339,000

84   B

Ledger account balance	£
Balance per ledger account	260
Cash discount disallowed	80
Adjusted ledger account balance	340

Supplier's statement	£
Balance per supplier's statement	1,350
Less:	
Goods returned	(270)
Cash in transit	(830)
Revised balance	250

Unreconciled difference = (£340 – £250) = £90

85   C

To record the purchase initially, the trade discount is deducted from the purchase price, but not the settlement discount. This will only be deducted when and if the early payment is made and the discount is taken.

86   B

	£
Net wages paid	12,450
Add back deductions:	
Income tax	2,480
Employees' National Insurance contributions	1,350
Pension contributions by employees	900
Gross wages	17,180

87   A

In the books of Y, if there is a debit balance of £1,250 on the account of X, this means that the balance represents an asset, i.e. X is a debtor of Y and owes Y £1,250.

88   A

A trial balance in a manual accounting system is a starting point for preparing the financial statements (but does not provide a summary of these statements). It should prove that total debit balances and total credit balances are equal, and so that the ledgers are arithmetically accurate. It will reveal the existence of errors if total debts and total credits are not equal, but will not show how the errors have been made. It cannot prove the accuracy of individual ledger accounts.

89   A

The invoice of $2,000 and the payment of $600 are differences arising from differences in the timing of recording the accounting entries in the accounts of DEF and M. These are easily explained and should be taken out in the reconciliation.

	$
M statement balance	3,000
DEF purchase ledger account balance	2,000
M statement balance higher by	1,000
Invoice in M's statement, not in DEF accounts	(2,000)
Payment in DEF's accounts, not on M's statement	600
Unexplained difference: DEF balance higher by:	(400)

90   A

Debtors control account

	$		$
Opening balance	80,000	Bank	100,000
Sales	90,000	Contra: creditors	6,000
		Sales returns	4,000
		Discounts allowed	10,000
		Closing balance	**50,000**
	170,000		170,000

91   D

	$
Net wages paid to employees	240,000
Tax deducted	24,000
Employees' national insurance	12,000
Pension scheme contributions	6,000
Charity donations	3,000
Gross wages	285,000
Employer's national insurance	14,000
Charge to profit and loss account for wages	299,000

92   B

Uniqueness of code numbers is an essential requirement. Answer D explains how codes might be used in an accounting system, but does not explain the key attributes of a code.

93   C

	$
Output tax	
$200,000 \times 15\%$	30,000
Input tax	
$161,000 \times (15/115)$	21,000
Net tax payable	9,000

CONTROL OF ACCOUNTING SYSTEMS

94   B

An error of principle occurs when an item is incorrectly classified and posted to the wrong type of account, for example when the purchase of plant and machinery (a fixed asset) is debited to the purchases account.

95   C

For example, an error of commission would occur if an expense for building rental was debited to the telephone expenses account. Both accounts are expense accounts, but the wrong expense account has been debited.

96   C

The main purpose of an audit is to determine that the accounts show a true and fair view of the financial state of the organisation.

97   D

A spreadsheet package could be used for any of the options, but is most suitable for dealing with the 'what if' situation of budget preparation.

98   B

Entering the wrong amount is an error of original entry. Not recording an entry is an error of omission. Recording entries in the wrong account is an error of commission. An error of principle is where an item is recorded in the wrong type of account.

99   D

The directors of a company have the responsibility for the accuracy of the accounts.

100 C

An error of principle breaks the 'rules' of an accounting principle or concept, for example incorrectly treating revenue expenditure as capital expenditure. The purchase of a fixed asset should be debited to a fixed asset account, not to the purchases account.

101 B

External auditors have to carry out their own duties, such as interpreting the results of a debtors circularisation. Internal auditors can support the work of the external auditors, for example by drawing up the letters in a debtors circularisation that the external auditors must post.

102 A

A computerised accounts package can be used for any of the purposes given, although the most useful in terms of improved accuracy and efficiency is the maintenance of the ledger accounts.

103 A

An error of original entry involves the wrong amount being entered in both accounts involved in the double entry. B is an error of commission and C is an error of principle. D is an error that would be revealed by the trial balance.

104 C

A total exemption from the requirement to have an external audit is given by section 249A of the Companies Act 1985 to small companies.

105 D

This responsibility is emphasised, in the case of listed companies, in the Combined Code on corporate governance. The responsibility for internal controls rests with the directors. If the company has an internal audit unit or department, the internal auditors will check internal controls but are not responsible for them.

106 B

Economy, efficiency and effectiveness are the 'three Es' of value for money audits.

107 C

Segregation of duties means that the work done by one person effectively acts as a check on the work done by someone else, reducing the risk of fraud or error.

108 A

An error of transposition occurs when either the debit or the credit side of a double entry (but not both) is written incorrectly, for example as $12,435 instead of $12,345. This will mean that total debit balances and total credit balances will not be equal. Omissions do not make the total debits and total credits unequal, because both the debit and the credit entry have been missed out. Errors of principle occur when a debit or credit entry is entered in the wrong account, but total debits and total credits will not be unequal as a result.

109 D

The principal duty of an external auditor is to provide a report to the shareholders.

110 D

The definition of an audit trail is the trail of a transaction from source document to financial statement.

111 D

The duty of the auditors is to prepare a report for the shareholders of the company, in which they give an opinion as to whether the financial statements give a true and fair view.

112 C

External auditors are appointed by the shareholders to report on the stewardship of directors. The directors are responsible for the financial statement, so it is they who will adjust for any errors found by the auditors.

113 C

A bank reconciliation can be used to detect errors in the cash book.

114 B

External auditors may rely on evidence provided by internal auditors.

115 B

A suspense account is needed when, as a result of an accounting error, total credit balances and debit balances will not be equal to each other.

Error 1. The entry should have been Credit Bank, Debt Motor Vehicles account. Instead, it was recorded as Credit Bank, Credit Motor Vehicles account. A suspense account is needed.

Error 2. The entry should have been Debit Bank, Credit Brown, but was recorded as Debit Bank, Credit Green. Total credits and debits will be equal, so no suspense account needed to correct the error.

Error 3. The entry has been recorded as: Credit Bank £9,500, Debit Rent £5,900. Credits and debits are unequal, so a suspense account is needed.

Error 4. The transaction has been recorded as Credit Debtors, Debit Discounts Received, but should have been recorded as Credit Debtors, Debit Discounts Allowed. Total credits and debits will be equal, so no suspense account is needed to correct the error.

Error 5. An omission of a transaction does not need a suspense account to correct it.

116 B

By crediting £40 to the Discounts Allowed account, when the discount should have been debited to the account, discounts allowed have been reduced by £40 when they should have been increased by £40. As a result of this error, profit has been overstated by $2 \times £40 = £80$.

117 C

Error 1. Total sales and total debtors have been recorded £370 too much.

Error 2. Total debtors has been recorded (£940 - £490) £450 too little.

As a result of these two errors, total debtors have been under-recorded by £450 - £370 = £80. The errors have not affected the accounts of individual debtors.

118   A

Think of the other side of the double entry that is needed to correct the error. This will help you to decide whether the entry in the suspense account should be a debit or a credit entry.

Error 1.   To correct , we must debit gas account £180, therefore credit suspense account.

Error 2.   To correct, we need to debit discounts received £50 and debit discounts allowed £50, so we must credit the suspense account with 2 × £50.

Error 3.   To correct, we need to credit interest receivable, therefore we debit suspense account.

Suspense account

	£		£
Balance (balancing figure)	210	Gas expense	180
Interest received	70	Discounts allowed	50
		Discounts received	50
	280		280

119   D

Discounts received should be recorded as:

Debit Creditors

Credit Discounts received.

Here, the discount has been debited instead of credited, so that the balance in the discounts received account is 2 × £200 = £400 too low. To correct, we must:

Credit Discounts received £400

Therefore Debit Suspense account £400.

120   B

The wording of this question can make it quite difficult, but the correct answer might be identified quickly.

Item B   Discounts allowed should be debited, therefore there is no error. If there is no error, we do not need a suspense account.

Item A   This is an error where a debit entry has been incorrectly recorded as a credit balance.

Item C   This might cause you a problem. If the bad debt has been omitted entirely, and no accounting entry has been made, there can be no suspense account entry. Here, it would seem that the debtors balance has been reduced for the bad debt (credit Debtors) but the bad debt expense account has not recorded the bad debt. If so, credits exceed debits and a suspense account entry is needed.

Item D   The error in item D makes total debits higher by £180. These will therefore cause an entry in the suspense account.

121 C

The error you should look for is one where the correction will require:

Debit Suspense account

Credit the other account containing the error.

PAYE and National Insurance deductions are liabilities, payable to the tax authorities. If they have been recorded twice, the credit balance is too high, and the correction will need a debit entry in this account.

The contra entry has credited both the control accounts, and to correct this will require a debit entry in the account containing the error (the purchase ledger/creditors control account).

Closing stock should be a debit entry, and so a debit is needed to correct the error.

A balance for an accrual is a credit balance, but has been recorded incorrectly as a debit balance. To correct the error, the telephone expense account must be credited, and so the suspense account will be debited.

122 D

The error has been to debit the debtor account and credit the supplier (creditor) account, instead of debiting the supplier account and crediting the debtor account. As a result debtors are over-stated by 2 × £270 = £540, and creditors are over-stated by £540. The error should be corrected, but sales and purchases are unaffected, so profit is unaffected. Total assets (debtors) and total liabilities (creditors) are both £540 too high, so that net assets are unchanged.

123 A

To decide what entries are needed in the suspense account, you should think about the entry in the other account that is needed to correct the error. The entry in the suspense account is then the other side of the double entry. For example, stock (an asset) should be a debit balance, so to correct the error, we need to debit the stock account and credit suspense account. Similarly, VAT payable should be a credit balance, and to record the missing VAT, we need to credit the VAT account, debit suspense account.

Suspense account

	£		£
Balance (balancing figure)	2,050	Stock (1,475 + 1,745)	3,220
Telephone expense (2 × £190)	380		
VAT (£5,390 - £4,600)	790		
	3,220		3,220

124 A

The VAT balance for purchases should be a debit balance, because the money is recoverable from the tax authorities. The VAT recoverable has been recorded as a credit entry (liability) instead of a debit entry, so to make the correction, we need to debit the VAT account by 2 × £3,079 = £6,158. The correction is Debit VAT £6,158, Credit Suspense account £6,158.

125 £14,600

	£
Profit as recorded	10,200
Reduce revenue expenditure	3,000
Increase revenue receipts	1,400
Correct net profit	14,600

126 B

If the suspense account shows a credit balance, the correcting entry to clear the account must be Debit Suspense account £130, credit the account with the error £130.

Purchases have been over-stated by £130, and to correct this, we need to credit the Purchases account (and so debit Suspense account) with £130.

Omissions of transactions (item A and possibly item C) do not affect total debits and credits. If item C means that total debtors have been reduced by the bad debt, but the bad debts account does not yet show the bad debt, the correcting entry would be to debit the Bad debts account and credit Suspense account. The error in item D leaves total debits and credits equal.

127 A

Computer equipment (an asset) will be over-stated. Stationery costs (an expense) will be under-stated, which means that profit will be over-stated.

128 C

Expenses are recorded from the petty cash book by debiting the relevant expense account in the nominal ledger with the total of expense in each of the analysis columns. If the totals in the analysis columns are £20 too low, the debit entries in the expense accounts will be too low. This will make the credit balances in the trial balance higher by £20.

129 C

The trial balance will fail to balance when a transaction is recorded but without matching debit and credit entries.

Item A   has been incorrectly recorded as Debit Machine repairs, Credit Creditors.

Item B   has been recorded incorrectly as Debit Bank, Credit Creditors.

Item C   has been recorded as Debit Sales returns, Debit Debtors, so this is the answer to the question.

Item D   is not clear, because depreciation could refer to either the depreciation charge for the period or the accumulated depreciation (provision for depreciation). Since item C is a correct answer, you needn't worry too much about the meaning of item D.

130 D

A involves too many debits, so the suspense account would have a credit balance.

B is the correct double entry, so no suspense account would be raised.

C involves a debit to the debtors control account £100 less than the true debtors figure obtained by totalling the sales ledger accounts, so again a suspense account would be a credit balance.

D involves a credit to the creditors control account £100 less than the true creditors figure, so a suspense account would have a debit balance.

131 A

As a result of the error, petrol expenses have been under-stated by (50 – 5) $45. When petty cash was topped up, the amount of cash drawn from the bank was $45 less than it should have been, and the actual petty cash balance is therefore only $705 rather than $750 – i.e. too low by $45. There is no trial balance imbalance, although there is an error in the accounts. The error is that the petty cash is overstated in the accounts by $45 (at $750 rather than the actual $705) and petrol expense shave been under-stated by $45. One debit balance (petty cash) is too high and the other (petrol expenses) is too low.

132 A

Financial controls are intended primarily to minimise the risk of fraud and error. They should have the consequence of both improving efficiency and reducing the audit fee. They are also likely to reduce the likelihood of breaching various legal requirements. However, answers B, C and D are not the main reason for financial controls.

133 A

Customers are paying on time, presumably, and so answer C cannot be correct. The problem appears to be that cheques are not being banked promptly, and so the cashier should be told to put the matter right. Delayed banking means inefficient cash management, and either a higher bank overdraft or a delay in receiving cash that could be put to other uses (e.g. earning interest). Senior management should be informed of the problem, but there is no reason to suspect that the delays in banking are connected in any way to fraud.

134 B

The answer to this question can be debated. Segregation of duties provides an internal control that minimises the risk of fraud and error. Answers C and D are not correct, because the process of carrying out a bank reconciliation and extracting a trial balance should reveal the existence of errors. Answer B is preferred, because segregating these duties reduces the risk of accounts being created and maintained for bogus customers or suppliers., or for incorrect payment details being entered in both the individual ledger accounts and the nominal ledger control account. In practice, a common feature of large accounting departments is the segregation of the sales ledger and the purchase ledger work. However, although this should improve efficiency, it does not obviously reduce the risk of fraud or error.

135 B

Total debits exceeds total credits, so the suspense account is opened with a credit balance of $2,300, to bring the totals into equality.

As a result of the first error, cash (debit balance) is under-stated by $600, and the correction is therefore Debit Cash, Credit Suspense account.

To correct the second error, we need:

  Credit Discount received $400

  Debit Suspense account $400, and

    Credit Interest payable $400

    Debit Suspense account $400.

The question is not well-worded in its description of the third error, and the nature of the error is not clear. It is assumed here that the error has been to Credit Sales instead of crediting the Disposal of fixed asset account. If this is the case, there is no adjustment in the Suspense account when the error is corrected (by Debit Sales, Credit Disposal account).

Suspense account

	$		$
Discounts received	400	Opening balance	2,300
Interest payable	400	Bank	600
Closing balance c/d	2,100		
	2,900		2,900
		Opening balance b/d	2,100

PREPARATION OF ACCOUNTS: ACCRUALS AND PREPAYMENTS, STOCKS, DEBTORS AND FIXED ASSETS

136 £1,350

The prudence concept states that stock should be valued at the lower of cost and NRV. This should be for each item of stock individually, rather than for stocks in total. Here, stock should be valued at £750 for X and £600 for Y.

137 A

	£
5 months at (£24,000/12) per month	10,000
7 months at (£30,000/12) per month	17,500
Annual rent expense	27,500

138 A

Cash sales do not affect debtors.

Discounts received affect creditors, not debtors.

The provision for doubtful debts does not affect the amount of debtors, but specific bad debts written off do affect debtors.

Debtors account

	£		£
Opening balance b/d	37,500	Discounts allowed	15,750
Sales (credit sales)	357,500	Bad debts written off	10,500
		Bank (balancing figure)	329,750
		Closing balance c/d	39,000
	395,000		395,000
Balance b/d	39,000		

139 A

The profit and loss account is a part of the double entry accounting system in the nominal ledger. When the profit for a period is being calculated, two double entry transactions to record are:

Credit Stock account (opening stock)

Debit Profit and loss account.

Debit Stock account (closing stock)

Credit Profit and loss account.

140 D

A fixed asset register is a detailed schedule of fixed assets, and is not another name for fixed asset ledger accounts in the nominal ledger.

141   £3,900

The best estimate of electricity expenses to accrue for June 20X4 is 1/3 × £600 = £200.

Electricity expenses account

	£		£
Bank	4,000	Opening balance b/d	300
Closing balance c/d	200	Profit and loss account	3,900
	4,200		4,200
		Opening balance b/d	200

142   C

The accrual for May and June 20X3 is assumed to be 2/3 × £840 = £560.

Electricity expenses account

	£		£
Bank	600	Opening balance b/d	300
Bank	720		
Bank	900		
Bank	840		
Closing balance c/d	560	Profit and loss account	3,320
	3,620		3,620
		Opening balance b/d	560

143   A

When a debt is written off as bad, the transaction is recorded as:

Debit Bad debts account (expense)

Credit Debtor account.

Any subsequent change to the provision for doubtful debts should be dealt with as a separate matter.

144   £122,000

Remember that: Opening stock plus (Purchases minus Returns) – Closing stock = Cost of sales. Here, all the figures are given except the figure for purchases.

	£
Opening stock	12,000
Purchases (balancing figure)	122,000
Purchase returns	(5,000)
	129,000
less Closing stock	(18,000)
Cost of sales	111,000

145 A

Error 1. The fixed asset has been treated as a purchase expense, and this will add to the cost of sales. As a result, both gross profit and net profit will be £50,000 lower. (This question ignores the depreciation charge that would have been made for the fixed asset.)

Error 2. The closing stock of stationery has been treated as raw materials stock, but net profit will not be affected. However, raw materials closing stock is used to measure the cost of sales, whereas stationery stock is not. The cost of sales will therefore be £10,000 lower, and gross profit will be £10,000 higher.

Taking the two errors together, gross profit will be £40,000 lower and net profit £50,000 lower, ignoring whatever the depreciation charge on the fixed asset would have been.

146 B

	£
Payments for purchases	85,400
less: Invoices for opening stock	(1,700)
plus: Invoices due for fuel purchased	1,300
Purchases	85,000

	£
Opening stock	12,500
Purchases	85,000
	97,500
Closing stock	(9,800)
Cost of fuel – P & L account	87,700

147 A

The situation in the question is unusual because there is an opening accrual on the account, but a closing prepayment of 1/3 x £1,200 = £400.

Rent account

	£		£
Bank	4,000	Balance b/d (accrual)	300
		Profit and loss account	3,300
		Balance c/d (prepayment)	400
	4,000		4,000
Balance b/d	400		

148 C

The premium for the year 1 July 20X2 to 30 June 20X3 was £13,200 × 1/1.1 = £12,000.

Profit and loss account charge:

6 months at £12,000 plus 6 months at £13,200 = £6,000 + £6,600.

149 £5,000

Depreciable amount £(60,000 – 12,000)	£48,000
Expected life	4 years
Annual depreciation charge	£12,000
Depreciation each month	£1,000
Depreciation charge in the period (5 months)	£5,000

150 B

With FIFO, closing stock is the most recently purchased stock, therefore when prices are rising, closing stock will have a higher value than if the average cost method of stock valuation is used. Since closing stocks will be valued higher, the cost of sales will be lower and the profit will be higher.

151 A

Debtors (5% of £2 million) = £100,000.

Required provision for doubtful debts (4% of £100,000) = £4,000.

Current provision for doubtful debts = £4,000 × ¾ = £3,000.

Increase in provision = £1,000.

An increase in the provision for doubtful debts reduces profits.

152 B

The cost of the asset to the buyer is the fair value of the goods given in exchange, which is the cost of those goods, £10,000.

153 A

Accumulated depreciation at the time of disposal = (3 years) 3 × 20% × £12,000 = £7,200.

Net book value at time of disposal £12,000 - £7,200 = £4,800.

Trade-in value of asset disposed of = £5,000.

Profit on disposal = £5,000 - £4,800 = £200.

154 C

The question presumably refers to the valuation of stock of finished goods or part-finished work in progress in a manufacturing business. Inward carriage costs (i.e. the costs of delivery of materials and components purchased from suppliers) are included in stock costs. Work in progress and finished goods should also include a share of production overhead costs.

155 A

The charge for bad and doubtful debts is the actual amount of bad debts written off plus the increase in the provision for doubtful debts, or minus the decrease in the provision.

	£
Provision at end of year (5% of £120,000)	6,000
Provision at start of year	9,000
Decrease in provision	(3,000)
Bad debts written off	5,000
Charge to P & L account	2,000

156 D

Depreciable amount £(52,000 – 4,000)	£48,000
Expected life	8 years
Annual depreciation charge	£6,000
Number of years' depreciation (20X2 – 20X6)	5
Accumulated depreciation at time of disposal	£30,000
	£
Cost	52,000
Accumulated depreciation at time of disposal	30,000
Net book value (NBV) at time of disposal	22,000
Disposal price	35,000
Profit on disposal	13,000

157   £15,525

	£
Purchase price	15,000
Transportation cost	1,500
Installation cost	750
Cost of fixed asset	17,250
Depreciation (10%)	1,725
NBV	15,525

158   C

The cost of manufactured goods should include the cost of the raw materials, including carriage inwards costs, plus conversion costs. Conversion costs are the cost of manufacturing labour and the cost of production overhead. Together, these are the costs of getting the products into their current condition. Carriage outwards and the costs of storage of finished goods should not be included, because they are costs incurred after the manufacture of the products is complete.

159   C

	Cost	Accum dep'n	NBV
	£000	£000	£000
Opening balance	860	397	
Disposal	(80)	(43)	
	780	354	
Purchase	180		
	960		
Depreciation (10%)		96	
		450	
NBV = 960 - 450			510

160

	£
Item (iii)	
Net realisable value of component P (200 × £208)	41,600
Less selling costs	(500)
	41,100
Units of component P: original cost (200 × £250)	50,000
Amount to write down	8,900

	£
Original valuation	72,857
(i) Overvaluation of nails: 8,000 × £0.99	(7,920)
(ii) Copying error has overvalued stock by (8,726 – 6,872)	(1,854)
(iii) Write-down of component P	(8,900)
Correct year-end stock value	54,183

161 A

The net realisable value of stock items is the selling price less the 4% commission payable.

	NRV	Lower of cost or NRV
	£	£
Henry VII	2,784	2,280
Dissuasion	3,840	3,840
John Bunion	1,248	1,248
		7,368

162 A

	NRV (discounted price)	Lower of cost or NRV
	£	£
Liszt	56.0	50.0
Delius	49.5	49.5
Offenbach	202.5	150.0
Bax	17.5	17.5
		267.0

163 C

Answer C is the most appropriate of the three definitions given, although it is not a strictly accurate definition.

164 A

The nominal ledger account for fixed assets shows a net book value that is £10,000 higher than the figure in the fixed assets register. This could be due to having omitted to deduct an asset with a NBV of £10,000 from the ledger. A fixed asset will have a NBV of £10,000 on disposal when it is sold for £15,000 and the profit on disposal is £5,000.

165 B

The accumulated depreciation at the start of the year is the difference between the cost of the assets and their net book value: £380,000 - £278,000= £102,000. The accumulated depreciation at the time of the revaluation is the depreciation at the start of the year (£102,000) plus the depreciation charge for the year up to the date of the revaluation. This is 2% × £380,000 = £7,600.

	£000
Freehold property at cost	380.0
Accumulated depreciation at time of revaluation (102 + 7.6)	109.6
Net book value at time of revaluation	270.4
Revaluation amount	411.0
Transfer to revaluation reserve	140.6

Answer B is the only one with this correct amount for the transfer to the revaluation reserve. The other book-keeping entries in answer B are also appropriate for recording the revaluation.

166 £62,210

	£
Sale value of asset	4,000
Loss on disposal	1,250
Net book value at time of disposal	5,250
Balance on fixed asset register before disposal	67,460
Balance on fixed asset register after disposal	62,210

167 C

1 Jan – 30 June: 3% of £380,000 × 6/12 = £5,700.

1 July – 31 December: 3% of £450,000 × 6/12 = £6,750.

Charge for the year: £5,700 + £6,750 = £12,450.

168 B

	£
Cost of asset	126,000
Depreciation to 31 October 20X3 (4/12 × 15%)	6,300
	119,700
Depreciation to 31 October 20X4 (15%)	17,955
	101,745
Depreciation to 31 October 20X5 (15%)	15,262
	86,483
Depreciation to 31 October 20X6 (15%)	12,972
	73,511
Depreciation to 30 September 20X7 (11/12 × 15%)	10,108
Net book value at time of disposal	63,403
Disposal price	54,800
Loss on disposal	8,603

169 C

Debtors (4% of £3 million)	£120,000
	£
Required provision for doubtful debts (3%)	3,600
Provision last year (£3,600 × 100/125)	2,880
Increase in provision	720
Bad debts written off	3,200
Bad debts recovered	(150)
Charge to P & L account	3,770

170 C

The calculations are a bit complex here. The general provision is 2% of the total debtors after deducting the specific provision. £13,720 therefore represents 98% of the total debtors after deducting the specific provision. This means that total debtors before deducting the specific provision are £13,720/0.98 = £14,000.

	£
Provision for doubtful debts at start of year:	
Specific	350
General (2% of £14,000)	280
	630
Required provision at end of year (3% of £17,500)	525
Reduction in provision (credit P & L account)	105

171 B

The receipt has been accounted for by:

Debit Bank, Credit Sales ledger control account.

It should have been accounted for as:

Debit Bank, Credit Bad debts.

(The debtor was removed from the accounts when the bad debt was written off. The receipt is the recovery of a bad debt, which is credited to the bad debts account.)

To correct the error:

Debit Sales ledger control account, Credit Bad debts.

172 £4,200

The charge to the profit and loss account is the bad debt written off (£4,000) plus the increase in the provision for doubtful debts (£200).

173 £950

Net realisable value = Sales price £1,200 less modification costs (£150) and selling costs (£100). NRV is therefore £950. Stock is valued at the lower of cost or NRV. Cost is £1,000, so the stock item should be valued at £950.

174 B

	Net realisable value	Lower of cost or NRV	Units	Value
	£	£		£
Basic	8	6	200	1,200
Super	8	8	250	2,000
Luxury	10	10	150	1,500
Total value				4,700

175 D

Do not include the road tax in the cost of the car. Road tax is a revenue expense item.

	£
Cost of asset	10,000
Depreciation 20X1 (25%)	2,500
	7,500
Depreciation 20X2 (25%)	1,875
	5,625
Depreciation 20X3 (25%)	1,406
	4,219
Depreciation 20X4 (25%)	1,055
Net book value at time of disposal	3,164
Disposal value	5,000
Profit on disposal	1,836

176   £2,950

	In	Out
Opening stock	50 at £40	
7 February	100 at £45	
14 February		50 at £40
		30 at £45
21 February	50 at £50	
28 February		60 at £45

Closing stock = 10 units at £45 (£450) plus 50 units at £50 (£2,500) = £2,950.

177   A

The asset disposed of had a net book value at the time of disposal = sales proceeds + loss on sale = £25,000 + £5,000 = £30,000.

	£
Net book value at 1 August 20X2	200,000
Net book value of asset disposed of	30,000
	170,000
Depreciation charge	20,000
Net book value at 31 July 20X3	150,000

178   B

Only purchased goodwill is recorded in the accounts of a business, not internally-generated ('inherent') goodwill. Purchased goodwill is classified as an intangible fixed asset.

179   A

You need to know the sales proceeds to calculate the length of ownership, or you need to know the length of ownership to calculate the sales proceeds. For example, this asset might have been sold after one year (NBV = £10,000) for £5,500, or it might have been sold after two years (NBV £8,000) for £3,500, and so on.

180   C

'Material' means of significance (typically 'of a significant monetary amount'). When assets have a long useful life but are of an insignificant value, it is simpler (and permissible) to write off the full purchase cost in the year of purchase. This avoids the need to calculate a depreciation charge each year, and maintain a fixed asset register for the items, and so on.

181   D

A provision for doubtful debts is a type of current liability. In the balance sheet, it is subtracted from debtors. An increase in a provision for doubtful debts will therefore reduce net current assets, i.e. it will reduce working capital.

182   B

Goods sold on a sale or return basis cannot be treated as a genuine sale until they have been sold on by the customer. It is necessary to eliminate the 'profit' on the sale. Stock should include the goods on sale or return, valued at cost. Debtors should exclude 'debts' for the sale-or-return goods.

	Stock	*Debtors*
	£	£
As originally stated	87,000	124,000
Adjust for sale or return goods	4,500	(6,000)
Balance sheet values	91,500	118,000

183   D

The reducing balance method charges more depreciation in earlier years than in later years. It is therefore appropriate to use for fixed assets such as motor vehicles that lose a large part of their value in the earlier years of their life.

184   A

	£
Bad debts written off (800 + 550)	1,350
Bad debt recovered	(350)
Reduction in provision for doubtful debts	(200)
Charge for bad and doubtful debts to P & L	800

185   C

Profit and loss account	$2,400 \times 7/12 = \$1,400$
Balance sheet prepayment	$2,400 \times 5/12 = \$1,000$

186   B

	$
Stock at valuation	13,000
Goods on sale or return at cost	6,000
Stock valuation	19,000

187   B

	$
Valuation at beginning of year	10,250
Purchases	3,450
Disposals	(2,175)
	11,525
Valuation at end of year	(8,000)
Depreciation	3,525

188 D

Rental income

	£		£
Balance brought down	1,400	Balance brought down	2,600
P & L (bal fig)	49,800	Bank	49,200
Balance carried down	2,400	Balance carried down	1,800
	53,600		53,600

189 B

The charge in the profit and loss account will be the amount of interest incurred from 1 January (when the loan was taken out) to 30 September (the year end) i.e. $9/12 \times 12\% \times £100,000 = £9,000$. This represents three interest payments.

However, as only two interest payments were made (1 April and 1 July) the third payment due to be made on 1 October, which relates to the three months to 30 September, will be accrued: $3/12 \times 12\% \times £100,000 = £3,000$

190 A

Rent

	£		£
Bank	1,800	Balance b/d	300
		P & L	1,200
		Balance c/d	300
	1,800		1,800

191 B

If the stock was not included in the original count of closing stock, closing stock will be increased by £1,000 (the lower of cost and net realisable value). Since closing stock is £1,000 higher, the cost of sales is £1,000 lower and profit £1,000 higher.

192 D

The closing stock of 12 items $(15 - 5 + 10 - 8)$ comprise

	£
10 items at £3.50 each	35.00
2 items at £3 each	6.00
Cost on a FIFO basis is	41.00

193 C

Stationery

	£		£
Balance b/f	165	Balance b/f	80
Stationery paid for	1,350	Profit & loss (balancing figure)	1,365
Balance c/f	70	Balance c/f	140
	1,585		1,585

194 C

	£
Rent: January – September 20X3 (9/12 × £1,200)	900
Rent: October – December 20X3 (3/12 × £1,600)	400
	1,300

195 D

Annual depreciation charge $\quad = \quad \dfrac{\text{Cost} - \text{Residual value}}{\text{Useful life}}$

$$= \quad \frac{£5,000 - £1,000}{4}$$

$$= \quad £1,000 \text{ pa}$$

Profit/loss on disposal $\quad = \quad$ Proceeds – Net book value on disposal

$\quad = \quad$ £1,600 – Net book value after 3 years

$\quad = \quad$ £1,600 – (£5,000 – £3,000)

$\quad = \quad$ loss of £400.

196 A

Net book value of asset disposed of was £5,500 (i.e. £4,000 plus £1,500) so adjusted fixed asset register balance is £47,500 - £5,500 = £42,000 which is £3,000 lower than the ledger accounts balance of cost £60,000 less depreciation £15,000 i.e. £45,000.

197 C

Date	In	Out	Balance
1 August			30 at £2 each: £60
5 August	50 at £2.40: £120		80 at £2.25: £180
10 August		40 at £2.25	40 at £2.25: £90
18 August	60 at £2.50: £150		100 at £2.40: £240
23 August		25 at £2.40	75 at £2.40: £180

198 B

Research costs cannot be capitalised. Development costs may be capitalised, subject to certain conditions.

199 A

	£	£
Machine cost		9,000
Accumulated depreciation after 3 years		
Year 1 9,000 × 30%	2,700	
Year 2 (9,000 – 2,700) × 30%	1,890	
	4,590	
Year 3 (9,000 – 4,590) × 30%	1,323	
		5,913
Net book value after three years		3,087
Sale value in Year 4		3,000
Loss on disposal		87

200 A

The aim of depreciation is to charge the consumption of value from the use of fixed assets over those time periods that benefit from the use of the asset. In historical cost accounting, this in effect means spreading the cost of the fixed asset in a fair way over its expected useful life.

201 A

When prices are rising, FIFO will give a higher valuation for closing stock, because the closing stock will consist of the most recently-purchased items. Higher closing stock means lower cost of sales and higher profit.

202 A

	$
Utility expenses paid	30,000
Less: Accruals brought forward at the start of the year	(3,600)
Less: Prepayment carried forwards at the year-end	(4,000)
Charge to the profit and loss account	22,400

203 C

	$
Prepayment brought forward at the start of the year	10,000
Payment during the year	36,000
	46,000
Less: prepayment carried forward at the year end	
(7 months, therefore $36,000 × 7/12)	21,000
Charge for insurance in the profit and loss account	25,000

204 C

Annual depreciation = $(40,000 – 10,000)/6 years = $5,000.

The machine was held for four years before disposal, giving accumulated depreciation of 4 × $5,000 = $20,000.

When the machine was sold, its net book value was $40,000 - $20,000 = $20,000. It was sold for $15,000, giving a loss on disposal of $5,000.

	$
Accumulated depreciation	20,000
Loss on disposal	5,000
Total charged over the life of the machine	25,000

205 C

The closing stock consists of (20 – 15 + 8 – 12) = 1 unit. With FIFO, this unit is valued at the cost of the most recently purchased item, i.e. at $6.

PREPARATION OF ACCOUNTS: FINANCIAL STATEMENTS AND RATIO ANALYSIS

206 B

Prime cost = direct manufacturing costs, in the case of a manufacturing company.

207 B

	£000
Opening stock of raw materials	45
Purchases of raw materials	150
	195
Less: closing stock of raw materials	(75)
	120
Manufacturing wages	50
Prime cost	170

208 £4.72M

	£ million
Fixed assets at cost	10.40
Accumulated depreciation	0.12
Net book value	10.28
Revaluation amount	15.00
Transfer to revaluation reserve	4.72

209 C

	£
Profit	8,000
Add depreciation (not a cash expense)	12,000
	20,000
Purchase of new fixed assets	(25,000)
Fall in cash balance	(5,000)

210 B

Discounts allowed are the balancing figure in the debtors account, after all the other figures have been entered in the account.

Debtors

	£			£
Balance b/d	800	Bank		6,730
Sales	6,800	Bad debts		40
		Discounts allowed		**280**
		Balance c/d		550
	7,600			7,600
Balance b/d	550			

211 D

Creditors

	£		£
Bank	542,300	Balance b/d	142,600
Discounts received	13,200	Purchases (balance)	**578,200**
Purchase returns	27,500		
Balance c/d	137,800		
	720,800		720,800
		Balance b/d	137,800

212 A

The figure for sales can be calculated by setting up a workings account for debtors, and calculating credit sales as the balancing figure. Having calculated credit sales, total sales equals credit sales plus cash sales.

It is assumed here that refunds to credit customers are refunds for overpayments.

Debtors (Workings account)

	£		£
Balance b/d	29,100	Cash from debtors	381,600
Refunds to customers	2,100	Expenses paid with cash from debtors	6,800
Sales (credit sales)	412,400	Bad debts	7,200
		Discounts allowed	9,400
		Balance c/d	38,600
	443,600		443,600

Total sales = Credit sales + Cash sales = £412,400 + £112,900 = £525,300.

213 D

Gross profit = 40% of sales.

Cost of sales = 60% of sales.

	£
Opening stock	17,000
Purchases	91,000
	108,000
Closing stock	(24,000)
Cost of sales	84,000
Sales = £84,000/0.60	140,000

214

Gross profit = 30% of sales.

Cost of sales = 70% of sales = 70% of £64,800 = £45,360.

	£
Opening stock	28,400
Purchases	49,600
	78,000
Cost of sales	45,360
Closing stock	32,640

215 A

	£000
Profit for the year	63,200
Depreciation	15,900
Profit on disposal of fixed asset	(7,000)
Fixed asset purchases	(18,000)
	54,100
Increase in stocks	(3,500)
Increase in debtors	(4,000)
Decrease in creditors	(1,600)
Net cash inflow	45,000

216 £18,950

	£
Sales	230,000
Money banked (160,000 + 50,000)	210,000
	20,000
Increase in debtors (3,000 – 2,000)	(1,000)
Increase in cash in till (100 – 50)	(50)
Money unaccounted for = stolen	18,950

217 A

	£
Purchases	20,000
Purchase returns	(2,000)
Change in stock	0
Cost of sales	18,000

	£
Sales	40,000
Sales returns	4,000
Net sales	36,000

Gross profit = £36,000 - £18,000 = £18,000.

218 C

	$
Cash in till at the end of the year	400
Cash banked, less cash from sale of the car (50,000 – 5,000)	45,000
Wages paid in cash	12,000
Drawings in cash from the till (2,000 x 12)	24,000
	81,400
Less: cash in the till at the start of the year	(300)
Sales for the year (all for cash)	81,100

219 D

The addition to share premium with the rights issue is 60,000 shares at (£1.20 - £0.25) each, i.e. £57,000.

	Share capital	Share premium
	£000	£000
At start of period	75	200
Rights issue	15	57
	90	257
Bonus issue	30	(30)
At end of period	120	227

220 D

Purchased goodwill is the difference between the price paid for a business and the fair value of its separable identifiable assets at the time of the purchase. For example, if a business buys another business for £2 million, and the fair value of its separately identifiable assets is just £1.5 million, there is purchased goodwill of £0.5 million. Purchased goodwill is an intangible fixed asset.

221 C

	£
Ordinary dividend (1,000,000 shares × £0.05)	50,000
Preference dividend (5% × £50,000)	2,500
Total dividend	52,500

222 B

Issued share capital and reserves are credit balances in the nominal ledger accounts (since capital balances are credit balances). The money raised is 200,000 × £1.30 = £260,000, of which £200,000 is share capital (nominal value) and £60,000 is share premium.

223 B

The loan was included as a current liability, but should be treated as a long-term liability. Correcting the error will reduce total current liabilities, and this will increase net current assets (= current assets minus current liabilities).

224 B

Salaries of company directors, loan interest and donations to charities are all expenses for a limited company, and come out of profit before taxation. Dividends, in contrast, are an appropriation of after-tax profit.

225 C

Giving customers more time to pay will result in an increase in debtors. An increase in debtors has a negative effect on cash flow, because it takes longer for the money to come in. A business can therefore make a profit but still suffer a fall in its bank balance due to an increase in debtors.

226 A

Preference shares are not regarded as equity capital (except perhaps that preference shares might be treated as equity for the purpose of some loan or bond documentation). Equity capital is therefore ordinary share capital plus reserves.

227 £43,080

	Change in assets	Change in liabilities	Change in capital	Change in working capital
	£	£	£	£
Pay creditors	(3,000)	(3,000)		0
Write off bad debt	(250)		(250)	(250)
Sell stock at a profit	(100)			
	230		130	130
				(120)
Opening work. cap.				43,200
Closing work. cap.				43,080

228 C

Ordinary share capital = 800,000 shares of £1.

Dividend = £120,000 = (£120,000/800,000) £0.15 per share.

229   C

A debenture is a secured fixed interest loan, repayable at a fixed date in the future. Interest on debentures is an expense in the profit and loss account. In practice, corporate bonds – which is a general term for loan securities issued by companies – are usually unsecured. In this respect they differ from most medium-term bank loans.

230   £93,000

Net cash outflow is assumed to mean the cash paid for new additions minus the cash received from disposals.

	£
Net book value of assets disposed of	15,000
Loss on disposals	6,000
Cash received from disposals	9,000
Cash paid for new additions	(102,000)
Net cash outflow	(93,000)

231   D

New purchase (additions) are given in the question as £2,000. The assets disposed of had a cost of £3,000 and accumulated depreciation at the time of disposal of £1,500. Their net book value at disposal was therefore £1,500. The profit on disposal was £500, so the cash received from the disposal was £2,000.

232   A

	£000
Operating profit	180
Depreciation	30
Profit on sale of fixed asset	(75)
	135
Increase in working capital (50 – 40)	(10)
Net cash flow from operating activities	125

233   D

Statement 1	is incorrect: net cash flow from operating activities is the same, whichever method of presentation is used.
Statement 2	is incorrect. Companies with high profits can be cash-negative, due to high spending on new fixed assets and/or a large build-up of working capital.
Statement 3	is incorrect. Profits and losses on fixed asset disposals are shown in the note to the cash flow statement that reconciles the operating profit to the net cash flow from operating activities.

234   D

Items added in this note include the depreciation charge for the period, any losses on disposals of fixed assets, reductions in stocks and debtors (including prepayments) and any increase in trade creditors (including accruals).

235

Disposals were £350,000.

Additions were £5,100,000. See workings below.

	£000
Net book value of assets disposed of	500
Profit on disposal	150
Fixed asset disposals	350

	£000
Net book value of assets at end of year	6,000
Net book value of assets at start of year	2,400
Increase in NBV	3,600
NBV of assets disposed of	500
	4,100
Depreciation charge for the year	1,000
Fixed asset additions	5,100

236 D

	£000
Profit for the year	18,750
Depreciation	1,250
Fixed asset purchases	(8,000)
Decrease in stocks	1,800
Increase in debtors	(1,000)
Increase in creditors	350
Net cash inflow	13,150

237 D

Stock turnover is the number of times stock is used up in the year. It is measured as the cost of stock consumed in the year (cost of goods sold) divided by the average stock level in the year, valued at cost.

238 A

Accepted 'norms' are 2.0 for the 'ideal' current ratio and 1.0 for the 'ideal' acid test ratio or quick ratio. However, these 'ideal' ratios are only a rough guide, since 'norms' vary greatly between companies in different industries. In this question, the current ratio is (1,390/420) 3.3 times and the acid test ratio is [(380 + 40)/420] 1.0 times. The current ratio is therefore high and the acid test ratio is 'ideal'.

239 D

The average debt collection period, measured as (debtors/sales) × 365 days, will increase when debtors rise but annual sales remain the same (or when debtors remain the same but annual sales fall). An increase in debtors without any increase in sales can happen as a result of poor credit control and debt collection procedures, or when debtors are abnormally high, perhaps due to a large credit sale or to seasonal sales being high.

A downturn in trade should result in a fall in both total debtors and annual sales, and there is no reason why the debtor collection period should change.

240   D

The ratio of stock to annual sales will increase when stock levels rise but there is no increase in annual sales. This could happen when stock control is poor and stocks are allowed to increase, or when there has just been a large purchase (temporarily increasing the stock level) or when stock levels are high due to high seasonal sales.

An increase in sales should result in some increase in stock levels, and there is no reason why the rate of stock turnover should change.

241   B

The answer calls for a simple definition of working capital.

242   C

Shareholders' return is usually measured as profit after tax, but in this question the figure for profit before tax must be used, since the profit after tax is not given.

Profit before tax = £200,000

Shareholders' equity = (in £000) 500 + 200 + 800 = £1,500,000.

Return on shareholders' equity = $(200/1,500) \times 100\% = 13.3\%$.

243   A

To compare like with like, we must measure ROCE as the profit before interest and taxation as a percentage of total share capital and long-term debt.

Return = £300,000.

Capital employed = £2,500,000.

Return on capital employed = $(300/2,500) \times 100\% = 12\%$.

244   D

Stock turnover should normally be measured by comparing the cost of average stock with the annual cost of sales. However, in this question you are asked how many days of stock are in hand at the end of the year, so you should use the figure for closing stock.

	£
Opening stock	1,750
Purchases	10,200
	11,950
less: Closing stock	1,950
Cost of sales	10,000

Days of sales in stock at the year-end = $(1,950/10,000) \times 365 = 71$ days.

245   A

The current ratio is the ratio of current assets to current liabilities. When a business has net current liabilities, the current ratio is less than 1.0.

A short-term loan will add to both current liabilities and to current assets (cash) by the same amount. When the current ratio is less than 1.0, an equal increase in current assets and current liabilities will alter the current ratio so that it is closer to 1.0 (although still less than 1.0). In other words, the current ratio will increase. Since the 'ideal' current ratio is 2.0, such an increase would improve the ratio.

246 B

An increase in debtors (answer C) and prepayments (answer D) would result in a reduction in cash flow, not an increase. Drawings also reduce cash flow (answer A).

The sale of fixed assets, either at a loss or a profit, will bring cash into the business, and could explain an increase in cash despite making a loss.

247 D

12% × 2 = 24%

$$\text{ROCE} = \frac{\text{Profit before interest and tax}}{\text{Sales}} \times \frac{\text{Sales}}{\text{Capital employed}}$$

248 A

Return on capital employed (ROCE) compares the profit before interest and tax with the total long-term capital of the company, both share capital (and reserves) and long-term debt. This contrasts with return on shareholder capital (ROSC), which compares profit after interest (and usually after tax as well) with share capital and reserves.

249 C

This is possibly a confusing question, because debtor days can be calculated in different ways. Strictly, debtor days should be calculated as (debtors including VAT/credit sales including VAT) × 365. This would give (23,500/50% of 235,000) × 365 = 73 days.

In practice, debtor days might be calculated as (debtors including VAT/total sales including VAT) × 365. This is because information is not always available about the division of total sales between cash sales and credit sales. In this question, debtor days would then be (23,500/235,000) × 365 = 37 days.

Even more often in practice, it is usual to measure debtor days approximately as (total debtors including VAT/total sales excluding VAT) × 365 days. This measurement is often used by stock market analysts, who can extract these figures easily from the published financial statements of a company. In this question, the debtor days would then be (23,500/200,000) × 365 days = 43 days.

This means that answers A, B and C could all be correct. However, given the information in the question, you are probably expected to compare like with like, i.e. debtors including VAT should be compared with credit sales including VAT.

250 C

When you are asked to calculate a gearing ratio, you ought to be given information about the basis on which the ratio is calculated, because there are different ways of measuring gearing. In particular, gearing might be measured as the percentage ratio of long-term debt to total shareholders' capital and reserves. Alternatively, gearing could be measured as the percentage ratio of (long-term debt plus some short term loans) to shareholders' capital and reserves.

In this question, the problem is deciding what to do about the overdraft of £50,000, which the company has apparently had for the second half of the year.

1   If gearing is measured as long term debt to share capital and reserves, the ratio would be (75/500) × 100% = 15%. This is not an option in the question.

2   If gearing is measured as (long term debt plus overdraft) to share capital and reserves, the ratio would be (125/500) × 100% = 25%. This is not an option in the question.

3   It might be assumed that since the overdraft has only been in place for one half of the year, just one half of it (£25,000) should be included in debt, together with the long-term debt of £75,000. This would give a gearing percentage of (100/500) × 100%. = 20%. This is an option in the question.

Although it is possibly not the best way of measuring gearing, it is the most plausible of the four available answers.

251   A

	£
Increase in stock	250
Decrease in bank balance	(400)
Increase in creditors	(1,200)
Change in working capital	(1,350)

252   C

When fixed assets are purchased on credit, creditors (= current liabilities) increase without any increase in current assets. Working capital is therefore reduced, in this case by £500.

When goods costing £3,000 are sold for £3,500, there is an increase in current assets and so an increase in working capital. (Stocks are reduced by £3,000 but debtors or cash increase by £3,500, and there is a profit of £500.) The sale of a fixed asset at a loss increases working capital, because cash is received from the sale and there is no other change in current assets or current liabilities.

253   D

This is another question that could be confusing because there are different ways of calculating the creditors' payment period. You should try to compare like with like in this type of question. Here, since creditors arise from purchases on credit, we should try to compare average creditors with purchases during the year. (A figure for purchases should be used rather than the figure for cost of sales.)

	£
Cost of sales	32,500
Add: Closing stock	3,800
	36,300
Less: Opening stock	(6,000)
Purchases	30,300

Creditors' payment period = (£4,750/£30,300) × 365 = 57 days

254   A

Gross profit = £60,000.

Mark-up = 50%.

Cost of sales = (£60,000/0.50) = £120,000.

Average stock = £(12,000 + 18,000)/2 = £15,000.

Stock turnover = £120,000/£15,000 = 8 times.

255   B

Gross profit margin = £800 = 33.33% of sales.

Sales = £800/0.3333 = £2,400.

Net profit = gross profit – expenses = £800 - £680 = £120.

Net profit percentage = net profit/sales = (£120/£2,400) × 100% = 0.05 or 5%.

256   A

Average stock = £(4,000 + 6,000)/2 = £5,000.

Stock turnover = Cost of sales/average stock = £24,500/£5,000 = 4.9 times.

257   C

This is another difficult question to answer, because all the possible answers seem sensible. Liquidity ratios can vary enormously between well-managed companies, particularly companies in different industries.

Many businesses operate efficiently with a bank overdraft. Similarly many businesses operate without difficulty with an acid test ratio of less than one. (Supermarkets, for example, have high stock levels but even higher amounts of creditors, and they operate comfortably with an acid test ratio well below 1.0.)

The correct answer, however, is C. The current ratio of the company is (2,900:1,100) 2.6 times, which is much higher than the industry norm of 1.8 times. This suggests that stock levels or debtor levels are unusually high for the industry, or creditor levels are unusually low. This is a possible sign of poor control over working capital, operating cash flows and liquidity.

258   A

There are different ways of measuring gearing. In particular, gearing might be measured as the percentage ratio of long-term debt to total shareholders' capital and reserves (including preference share capital). Alternatively, gearing could be measured as the percentage ratio of (long-term debt plus preference share capital) to ordinary share capital and reserves.

Answer A is a correct definition. Answer C is incorrect, because preference share capital cannot be included both above the line with long-term debt and below the line as part of shareholders' capital.

259   C

If the cost per unit goes down, but the sales price and sales quantity remain the same, the gross profit margin must go up.

The gross profit margin might go up if both cost per unit and sales price go up, but it might also fall, depending on the size of the rise in each. (Answer A is therefore incorrect.) When sales volume goes up, there need not be any change in the gross profit margin as a percentage, so answer B is inappropriate.

260   A

Gearing at 31.10.X3 = [15/(20 + 10 + 43)] × 100% = 21%.

Gearing at 31.10.X4 = [50/(30 + 20 + 36)] × 100% = 58%.

There has been an increase in gearing and as a result the financial risk for shareholders is higher.

261 B

20X8

Average stock	= (75 + 85)/2 = 80.
Cost of sales	= 1,250
Stock turnover	= 1,250/80 = 15.6 times.

20X9

Average stock	= (85 + 155)/2 = 100.
Cost of sales	= 1,300
Stock turnover	= 1,300/100 = 13 times.

Stock turnover has fallen. A reduction in the rate of stock turnover results in an increase in stock levels (unless there is also a fall in the cost of sales). This has a negative effect on cash flow and so has a possible detrimental effect on liquidity.

262 D

Since subscriptions in arrears are accounted for only when the payments are received, accruals of income can be ignored, and only prepayments of income (subscriptions received in advance) are relevant for calculating income for the year.

	$
Subscriptions in advance brought forward at 1 April 20X1	500
Subscriptions received	10,000
	10,500
Subscriptions in advance carried forward at 31 March 20X2	(600)
Subscriptions for the year to 31 March 20X2	9,900

263 B

	$
Subscriptions paid for 20X1	6,000
Subscriptions owing for 20X1	750
Subscription income for 20X1	6,750

264 B

This is a basic distinction that you need to be aware of. Income and expenditure accounts are the equivalent of profit and loss accounts for non-profit making associations such as sports clubs.

265 D

	£
Subscriptions due for 20X8 (1,548 × 10)	15,480
Subscriptions for 20X8 paid in advance in 20X7: (27 × 10)	(270)
Subscriptions for 20X8 in arrears at the year end: (25 × 10)	(250)
Cash received for 20X8 subscriptions in 20X8	14,960
Cash received for subscriptions in arrears from 20X7: (52 × 8)	416
Cash received for subscriptions in advance for 20X9: (72 × 12)	864
Cash received during 20X8	16,240

266 A

Cash was received in the year for £14,640/£12 = 1,220 annual subscriptions.

Annual subscription payments received in the year	1,220
Subscriptions received in advance for 20X8 during 20X7	15
	1,235
Receipt of arrears from 20X7	(18)
Receipt of advance payments for 20X9	(17)
Cash received for 20X8 subscriptions	1,200
Total number of members	1,200
Subscriptions in arrears at 30 September 20X8	0

267 B

	£
Cash received for subscriptions in 20X5	12,500
Receipt of arrears from 20X4	(800)
Receipt of advance payments for 20X6	(400)
Cash received for 20X5 subscriptions	11,300
Add: subscriptions in arrears for 20X5	250
Subscription income for 20X5	11,550

268 C

It is a statement for a non-profit making organisation, and similar to a profit and loss account.

269 A

Life membership fees are usually dealt with by crediting the total to a life membership fees account and transferring a proportion each year to the income and expenditure account. This is consistent with the accruals or matching concept in accounting.

270 B

	£
Subscriptions received in the year	4,750
Subscriptions paid in advance at start of the year	90
	4,840
Subscriptions in arrears at start of year, paid in the current year (150 – 40)	(110)
	4,730
Subscriptions paid in advance at start of the year	(75)
Income for the year	4,655

271 B

	£
Cash received for subscriptions	12,450
Receipt of arrears from last year	(50)
Receipt of advance payments for next year	(120)
Cash received for current year subscriptions	12,280
Add: subscriptions paid in advance last year for this year	75
Subscription income for the current year	12,355

272 B

The accumulated fund is a term used in not-for-profit organisations for the total of the lower half of the balance sheet, which represents the net assets of the organisation at book value. (Note that this would not be the case if there was a special fund represented by any special fund assets.) The excess of income over expenditure for a period is transferred to the accumulated fund.

273 A

The mark-up = 20%, so the cost of sales = (100/(100 + 20)) = 100/120 × Sales.

Cost of sales = £300,000 × 100/120 = £250,000.

	£	£
Sales		300,000
Opening stock	55,000	
Purchases	230,000	
	285,000	
Closing stock (balancing figure)	(35,000)	
Cost of goods sold		250,000
Gross profit		50,000

274 C

	£
Sales	480,000
Gross profit 33.33% of sales (= mark-up of 50%)	160,000
	320,000
Stock adjustment: 40,680 – 36,420	4,260
Purchases	324,260
Creditors adjustment: 33,875 – 29,590	4,285
Cash	319,975

275 A

	£
Direct materials	8,000
Direct labour	10,000
Prime cost	18,000

276 D

Gross profit minus expenses equals net profit, so gross profit must equal net profit plus expenses. Answer B gives the cost of sales, not the gross profit.

277 C

	£	£
Total receipts		85,000
Receipts from cash sales		(5,000)
Receipts from debtors (credit sales)		80,000
Closing debtors (current year sales)	9,000	
Opening debtors (previous year sales)	(10,000)	
		(1,000)
Credit sales in the year		79,000

278 B

The goods should not be recognised as a sale until the purchaser no longer has the right to return them. So the sale should not be recognised until 10 January 20X4. The matching expenses of the sale should only be charged when the sale is recognised, under the accruals concept.

So both the revenues and the expenses should be recognised in 20X4.

279 D

	£	£
Opening stock		12,000
Purchases (balancing figure)	122,000	
Less: Purchase returns	(5,000)	
		117,000
		129,000
Closing stock		(18,000)
Cost of goods sold		111,000

280 D

A higher figure for closing stock means a lower value for the cost of manufactured goods completed.

281 B

ROCE is here taken to be operating profit/Share capital and reserves

$= (1,500/4,000) \times 100\% = 37.5\%$.

282 D

Fixed asset turnover ratio = Sales/Fixed assets

$= 5,000/3,000$

$= 1.67: 1$

283 B

Quick ratio = (Current assets excluding stock)/Current liabilities

$= (1,250 – 300)/250$

$= 950/250$

$= 3.8: 1$

284 B

To record the loss of the car through the fixed asset disposal account, the disposal account would be debited with the net book value of the asset ($8,000) and credited with the proceeds, which in this case would be a debtor for insurance money ($6,000). The balance of $2,000 would have been written off as a net loss. When the insurance company eventually pays $6,500, which is $500 more than expected, $6,000 is recorded as a payment by the debtor and the remaining $500 will be taken as income to the profit and loss account. The only answer that provides for this to happen is answer B.

285 C

	$
Opening work-in-progress	240,000
Manufacturing costs:	
Prime cost	720,000
Factory overhead	72,000
	1,032,000
Closing work-in-progress	(350,000)
Factory cost of completed output	682,000

Section 4

ANSWERS TO PRACTICE QUESTIONS

CONCEPTUAL AND REGULATORY FRAMEWORK

1   D

(i)   An accounting system in which assets and liabilities, and items the cost of sales, are all valued at their original cost, and not at their replacement cost or current value.

(ii)   In HCA, land and buildings are valued at their original purchase cost, regardless of their current value, and depreciation of buildings is based on this historical cost.

(iii) NRV is the amount that should be obtained from the asset through disposal or use. It is the asset's sale value less any further processing and selling costs.

(iv)   The NRV of a stock item is the sale value of the item less any further processing and selling costs up to the point of sale.

(v)   CCA is an accounting system in which assets and liabilities, and the cost of sales, are all valued at their current cost/value, rather than at their historical cost.

(vi)   The economic value of an asset is the value of all the future economic benefits that the assets will be expected to earn or obtain.

(vii) The balance sheet value of assets will be higher than under HCA. The cost of sales will also be higher, and so the reported profit will be lower, than with HCA.

(viii) Avoiding a reduction in the value of the business net assets (i.e. capital), by ensuring that no profit is recorded unless net asset values have risen during the period.

2   BUSINESS WORLD

(a)

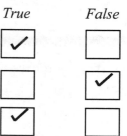

	True	False
Corporations, partnerships and sole traders are all forms of business entities.	✓	
For accounting purposes, the individual business is **not** regarded as an entity in its own right.		✓
A registered company has a separate legal personality.	✓	

(b)   Equity investors

Trade creditors

Inland Revenue

(*Note:* There are many examples. Any appropriate three would earn marks.)

(c) (i) Financial accounting concerns the production of the main **financial statements** mainly for **external** users.

(ii) Management accounting concerns the production of **information** mainly for **internal** users.

(iii) The **profit and loss account** reflects the performance of a company over a period. It shows the **movement** (or changes) between the position at the beginning and at the close of the period.

(iv) Current liabilities are amounts **owed** by the business, payable within **one year** of the balance sheet date.

(v) Capital expenditure is expenditure on acquiring **fixed** assets. Revenue expenditure is expenditure on items of **stock or expenses**.

3 GAAP

(a) Generally Accepted Accounting Practice

(b) (i) Assets and liabilities should not be offset against one another.

(ii) Transactions are accounted for in accordance with their economic substance rather than their legal form.

(iii) Information is material if its omission or misstatement would influence the decisions of users relying upon the accounts.

Income is recognised when either realised in cash or almost certain to be realised in cash.

(v) Accounting statements should contain only information that complies strictly with the specific requirements of the user.

(vi) Accounting statements should be prepared with the minimum amount of personal bias and the maximum amount of overall objectivity.

(vii) Every transaction has two effects.

(viii) Only items which can have a monetary value attributed to them will be recorded in the accounts.

(ix) The directors of the company are stewards of the assets of the company which the shareholders own.

4 CONCEPTS

(i) *Prudence*

The prudence concept states that revenue and profits are not anticipated, but are recognised only when realised.

(ii) *Realisation*

Revenue and profits are not anticipated, but are recognised only when they are realised in the form of cash or other assets.

(iii) *Stewardship*

The stewardship concept states that the directors of the company are stewards of the assets of the company, which the shareholders own.

(iv)   *True and fair view*

The figures in the accounts have been accurately arrived at when possible (true) and when judgement is needed it has been exercised without bias (fair).

(v)   *Neutrality*

This is the same as objectivity. In other words, it is the intention that financial statements should be free from bias.

(vi)   *Money measurement*

Only assets and liabilities that are capable of being measured in monetary terms will be included in the balance sheet of a company.

(vii)   *Accruals*

Income should be matched with related expenditure and both income and expenditure should be included in the period in which it is incurred.

(viii)   *Consistency*

Items in the accounts should be treated in the same way in each accounting period and similar items should be treated in the same way.

5   DEFINITIONS

(a)   (i)   An asset is a right (or other access) to future economic benefits controlled by an enterprise as a result of a past transaction or event.

(ii)   A liability is an obligation of an enterprise to transfer economic benefits, as a result of a past event or transaction.

(iii)   A capital receipt is a receipt of a long-term or 'capital' nature that will provide benefits over more than one accounting period.

(iv)   Capital expenditure is expenditure on acquiring, making or improving fixed assets (or acquiring another business).

(b)   (i)   Stock. Stock has been purchased (a past transaction) and provides access to future sales income, which is an economic benefit.

(ii)   Trade creditors. An enterprise owes money to its suppliers and is under an obligation to pay them (transfer economic benefits) as a result of past purchases.

(iii)   Receipt of cash from a share issue. This transaction adds to the capital of a company and provides long-term benefits.

(iv)   Expenditure on new equipment or machinery. Equipment and machinery are fixed assets, and the cost of acquiring it is capital expenditure.

ACCOUNTING SYSTEMS

6   TANWIR

Capital

			£
	01/10/X9	**Bank**	**20,000**

Bank

		£			£
01/10/X9	**Capital**	**20,000**	03/10/X9	Rent payable	**1,200**
28/10/X9	**P Duncan**	**500**	05/10/X9	Office equipment	**5,000**
			25/10/X9	**A Jones (3,500 – 500)**	**3,000**
			31/10/X9	Balance c/d	**11,300**
		20,500			**20,500**
01/11/X9	Balance b/d	**11,300**			

Purchases

		£			
02/10/X9	**A Jones**	**3,500**			
18/10/X9	**A Jones**	**2,400**			

A Jones

		£			£
15/10/X9	**Returns outwards**	**500**	02/10/X9	**Purchases**	**3,500**
25/10/X9	Bank	3,000	18/10/X9	Purchases	2,400
31/10/X9	Balance c/d	**2,400**			
		5,900			**5,900**
			01/11/X9	Balance b/d	**2,400**

Rent payable

		£			
03/10/X9	**Bank**	**1,200**			

Office equipment

		£			
05/10/X9	**Bank**	**5,000**			

Sales

					£
			10/10/X9	**P Duncan**	**1,750**

P Duncan

		£			£
10/10/X9	**Sales**	**1,750**	28/10/X9	Bank	500
			31/10/X9	**Balance c/d**	**1,250**
		1,750			**1,750**
01/11/X9	Balance b/d	**1,250**			

Returns outwards

		£
15/10/X9	A Jones	**500**

7   BOOKS OF PRIME ENTRY

(a)   (i)   **Trade** discounts are adjustments between the stated price on the price list and the actual price being charged.

(ii)   **Cash or settlement** discounts are percentage allowances made to a debtor as an incentive to settle within the terms of the original scale.

(b)

		True	False
(i)	Trade discounts are recorded in the cash book.		✓
(ii)	Cash discounts are recorded in the cash book.	✓	
(iii)	The debtors' and creditors' ledgers form part of the double entry system.		✓
(iv)	The journal book is a book of prime entry.	✓	
(v)	The day books are not part of the double entry system.	✓	

(vi)   A debtors' ledger control account may contain the following totals for the period:

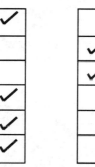

	True	False
- Sales (sales day book)	✓	
- Cash paid (cash book)		✓
- Discounts received (cash book)		✓
- Discounts allowed (cash book)	✓	
- Sales returns	✓	
- Bad debts expense	✓	

8   EMPLOYEES

Key answer tips

Required   -   Parts (a) and (b) are fairly straightforward. In part (c) you must give a possible solution to each weakness and in part (d) suggest additional controls.

Not required   -   Narrative for the journal entry.

(a)

		Dr	Cr
Dr	Total wages account (78,000 + 5,250)	**83,250**	
Cr	PAYE creditor account		**12,800**
Cr	NI creditor account (5,600 + 5,250)		**10,850**
Cr	Pension scheme creditor account		**4,600**
Cr	Wage creditor account (78,000 – 12,800 – 5,600 – 4,600)		**55,000**

(b) The amount to be debited to the profit and loss account for October is **£83,250**.

The balance sheet extract at 31 October 20X8 is:

Creditors: **Amounts falling due for payment within 12 months**:

	£
PAYE creditor	**12,800**
NI creditor	**10,850**
Pension fund creditor	**4,600**
Accrued wages	**55,000**
	83,250

(c) There appears to be no division of **duties** in the payroll department. Your duties as payroll administrator include preparing the payroll, receiving the overtime claim forms, inputting the data and making out the cheques. The opportunity for fraud such as **dummy employees** is therefore huge. There should be some division of labour introduced which could be done fairly easily by at the very least the cheques being prepared by another department such as the purchases ledger or the cashier.

The computer should have some form of **validation** checks for data that is obviously suspect. For example on this computer printout employee 1 has a gross wage of £6,000 which would be impossible with a maximum basic pay of £2,000 per month. The computer should be able to produce some sort of **exception** report highlighting any such figures.

There appears to be little control over overtime payments as the Overtime Report Form is submitted directly to you. An **appropriate** person should firstly authorise any overtime that is to be worked and the hours submitted on the Report Form should be checked to **attendance records** or job sheets.

(d) A batch processing system is where **similar** types of documents are collected together, such as sales invoices or in this case payroll details, and they are then input into the computer in **one batch**. The data is then used by the computer to update the relevant ledger accounts.

Any such input of data should have a number of controls associated with it known as **batch** controls. These include the **sequential** numbering of the documents which does appear to have happened here, each employee is given a sequential number. Prior to input there should also be a batch total calculated and batch header filled in. It is not possible to tell whether this has taken place.

However it is quite clear from the data for employee 1 that there is no **validation** procedure within the system. A **validation** procedure should check that the input is reasonable by comparing to **upper and lower** limits, that the data is current and that the accounts being updated do in fact exist.

CONTROL OF ACCOUNTING SYSTEMS

9 BH

Key answer tips

For part (a), you are required to describe a petty cash imprest system and to explain the purpose of it. This covers not only maintenance of the imprest system but also recording of the petty cash expenditure. For part (b), efficiency and control need to be discussed in the context of the day book system. For part (c), you need to work carefully through each figure deciding whether or not it appears in the sales ledger control account.

Take care with the VAT. The VAT inclusive amounts are required in the control account. Note also that no entry appears in the control account for the provision for doubtful debts.

(a) **Petty cash** is the actual cash that a business will have on its premises in order to meet small non-cheque payments by employees such as **travel costs and tea and coffee**.

An **imprest system** is where a predetermined amount of cash, say £100, is withdrawn from the business' bank account and put into the petty cash box in order to cover the following week's expenses. If an employee wishes to be reimbursed for cash that he has paid out on behalf of the business then that employee must fill out a pre-numbered **petty cash voucher**. Usually this voucher must also be supported by an invoice or receipt. The voucher must then be authorised by the appropriate person and then the employee will be reimbursed out of the petty cash box. The voucher will remain in the petty cash box. Therefore at any point in time the cash in the petty cash box and the vouchers should always total back to the imprest amount, in our case £100.

At the end of the week the total of the vouchers is determined and this amount is then withdrawn from the bank in cash in order to return the petty cash box to the **imprest** amount of £100.

The petty cash expenditure is recorded in the petty cash book from each of the vouchers. The amount of cash paid into the petty cash box to bring it back to the **imprest** amount is also recorded as a receipt in the petty cash book.

The main purpose of the imprest system is therefore to provide **control** over the cash held and to provide a means of reimbursing employees for cash expenditure on behalf of the business.

(b) (i) Debit   Purchases

       Credit   Creditors control

(ii) Debit   Debtors control

       Credit   Sales

(iii) Sales ledger

(iv) Purchases ledger

(c)

BH – Sales ledger control account

		£			£
1 Feb 20X7	Opening balance	**103,670**	1 Feb 20X7	Opening balance	**1,400**
	Sales	**175,860**		**Returns in**	**9,500**
	VAT on sales	**10,350**		Receipts	126,750
	Refunds	800		Discount allowed	**1,150**
	Bad debt written back	**300**		Contra	**750**
	Dishonoured cheques	**1,580**		**Bad debt written off**	**2,300**
28 Feb 20X7	Closing balance	840	28 Feb 20X7	Closing balance	**151,550**
		293,400			**293,400**
1 Mar 20X7	Opening balance	**151,550**	1 Mar 20X7	Opening balance	**840**

10   MLN

Key answer tips

When preparing the suspense account, make sure that you only include the errors that are one-sided entries. For part (c), you also need to consider which errors affect the profit and loss account.

You are not given the total of the individual customer balances so you need to work back to it from the control account balance. Item (6) is the purchase day book not sales so ignore it.

You need to realise that the treatment of the suspense account balance by applying the prudence concept means that, as a credit balance, it was included as a liability in the draft accounts rather than income.

(a)

Suspense account

		£			£
(1)	**Sales ledger control**	**1,248**		**Per trial balance**	**2,045**
(5)	**Bank charges**	**66**	(4)	**Telephones**	**9**
(7)	**Fixed asset disposal**	**740**			
		2,054			**2,054**

(b)

Sales ledger control account

		£			£
	Balance brought down	327,762	(1)	**Discount allowed**	**1,248**
(2)	**Sales**	**857**	(3)	**Contra (731 × 2)**	**1,462**
				Balance carried down	**325,909**
		328,619			**328,619**

Sales ledger listing

		£
	Balance per listing (balancing figure)	**325,052**
(2)	**Debtor not included**	**857**
	Adjusted listing (from control account)	**325,909**

(c)

		£	£
	Net profit per draft accounts	412,967	
(2)	**Add: Credit sales to SEC Ltd**	**857**	
			413,824
(4)	**Less: Telephone**	**9**	
(6)	**Purchases addition error**	**360**	
(7)	**Loss on disposal (740 – 800)**	**60**	
		429	
	Adjusted net profit		**413,395**

11 TD

Key answer tips

Part (a) (ii) The cost of getting a fixed asset into its correct working order is regarded as a capital cost and therefore capitalised as part of the cost of the fixed asset. (iii) If the supplier has noticed this then the discount will not be allowed and £150 must be added back to the creditors' account. (vi) This one is quite complicated to work out. Purchase returns had been overstated and sales returns understated but no other accounts affected so the total goes to the suspense account.

Part (c) is the challenging element here asking you to distinguish between errors which affected the gross profit (trading account) and those which affected the profit and loss account (net profit).

(a) **TD – Journal entries**

		Debit £	*Credit* £
(i)	Suspense account	**1,000**	
	Sales		**1,000**
(ii)	Plant at cost	**240**	
	Delivery costs		**240**
(iii)	Discounts **received**	**150**	
	JW	**150**	
(iv)	Stationery **stock (balance sheet)**	**240**	
	Stationery **account**		**240**
(v)	Suspense account	**500**	
	Purchases		**500**
(vi)	**Purchase returns**	**230**	
	Sales returns	**230**	
	Suspense account		**460**

(b)

Suspense account

		£			£
(i)	**Sales**	**1,000**	Balance per trial balance		1,040
(v)	**Purchases**	**500**	**(vi)**	**Returns in and out**	**460**
		1,500			**1,500**

(c)

		£
Gross profit – original		35,750
Add:	(i)	**1,000**
Add:	(v)	**500**
Less:	(vi)	**(460)**
Revised gross profit		**36,790**
Net profit – original		18,500
Add:	**Increase in gross profit**	**1,040**
Add:	(ii)	**240**
Less:	(iii)	**(150)**
Add:	(iv)	**240**
Revised net profit		**19,870**

12   MMM LTD

(a)

MMM Ltd - Profit and loss appropriation accounts

	£	£
	Year 1	*Year 2*
Profit before tax	48,800	55,000
Corporation tax	(6,500)	(8,000)
Profit after tax	42,300	47,000
Dividends **(18,000)**	**(31,200)**	
Transfer to reserves	**(5,000)**	**(5,000)**
Retained profit	**19,300**	**10,800**

(b)

MMM Ltd - Capital and reserves

	£	£
	Year 1	*Year 2*
Issued share capital	**360,000**	**390,000**
Share premium	**144,000**	**159,000**
General reserve	**5,000**	**10,000**
P & L account	**19,300**	**30,100**
	528,300	**589,100**

(c)

	True	*False*
The purpose of the internal audit is to provide an independent check on the stewardship function of the directors.	▦	✔
The external auditor reports to the directors of the company.	☐	✔

The auditor checks that the company has a proper system of accounting records that is adequate to produce a true and fair set of financial statements. ☑ ☐

The auditor will also attempt to discover any fraudulent activities which is a primary purpose of an audit. ☐ ☑

ACCRUALS, PREPAYMENTS, STOCKS, DEBTORS AND FIXED ASSETS

13 JOHN BARKER

(a) Income and expenses should be matched and dealt with in the period profit and loss account to which they relate.

(b) (i) **£1,100**

	£
1 January 20X8 to 30 November 20X8	1,000
Add: Accrual December 20X8 ($\frac{1}{3} \times £300$)	100
	£1,100

(ii) **£4,600**

	£
1/1/X8 to 31/3/X8 ($\frac{1}{4} \times £4,000$)	1,000
1/4/X8 to 31/3/X9	4,800
Less: Prepayment 1/1/X9 to 31/3/X9 ($\frac{1}{4} \times 4,800$)	(1,200)
	£4,600

(c)

	True	*False*
Accruals and prepayments never apply to items of miscellaneous income.	☐	☑
Accruals and prepayments are short-term in nature.	☑	☐

14 PROVISION

Key answer tips

Required - Follow through the instructions in the question regarding the provision. Note that you will need workings to determine the balance on the debtors account at the end of each year. Notice that as the provision has decreased at the end of year 2, the provision account is debited and the profit and loss account credited.

Not required - A separate bad debts expense account.

(a)

Provision for doubtful debts

20X1		£	20X1		£
31.12	**Sales ledger control a/c**	**600**	1.1	**Balance brought forward**	**1,000**
31.12	Balance c/f Step 2	1,470	31.12	P & L a/c (balancing figure)	1,070
		2,070			2,070
20X2			20X2		
31.12	P & L a/c (balancing figure)	520	1.1	Balance brought forward	1,470
31.12	Balance c/f Step 3	950			
		1,470			1,470

Workings

Step 1 Set up the provision account and enter each entry as required.

Step 2 Calculate the closing balance on debtors for year 1 (20,000 + 90,000 – 80,000 – 600 = £29,400). Therefore the closing provision should be:

£29,400 × 5% = £1,470

Step 3 Calculate the closing balance on debtors for year 2 (29,400 + 100,000 – 110,000 - 400 = £19,000). Therefore the closing provision should be:

£19,000 × 5% = £950

(b) The balance on the provision account is not a liability. It is a reduction in the asset (debtors) to account for the debts that may not be collected.

15 COST AND NRV

Key answer tips

Required - For part (a), a simple explanation of the four terms is required. For parts (b) and (c), however, you need to think more deeply about this method of stock valuation and you must mention the users of accounts.

Not required - Any explanation of how stock values are arrived at.

(a) (i) *Historical cost* - the original cost to the business of assets and expenses.

(ii) *Net realisable value* - the expected sale value of the asset in the ordinary course of business, less any costs of realisation.

(iii) The *prudence convention* - revenues should only be recognised when they are reasonably certain, but liabilities should be recognised when they are known.

(iv) The *consistency convention* - financial statements should be prepared within each period and from one year to the next such that they are comparable.

(b) It could be argued that the quotation is correct. Under this policy the same type of stock item may be valued in different ways in different years. However, what is really being applied is a consistent policy of prudence, therefore one can also argue that there is indeed consistency of treatment. Losses are always being recognised immediately and profit is not taken on stock until it is sold.

(c)   The main argument in favour of this policy is the argument of prudence. Users of the financial statements can be assured that the figure for stock has not been over-estimated given the nature of the stock itself and the type of business. Therefore loan creditors can be assured that the value for stock in the balance sheet is at least what the stock will actually realise and shareholders can be confident that any losses due to the condition of the items of stock have already been taken into account.

Under the prudence policy there is a deliberate bias towards understating assets and profits and this is unlikely to help in providing an accurate picture of the business. Also as argued in part (b) above, there is an element of inconsistency in this policy and perhaps it would be better either to value all stock at cost, regardless of future realisation value, or to value stocks at their total realisable value rather than a mixture of the two.

16   JAY LTD

(a)

	Receipts			Issues			Balance	
Date	Quantity	Price £	Value £	Quantity	Price £	Value £	Quantity	Value £
October								
1	120	8	960				120	960
3	180	9	1,620				300	2,580
4				120	8	960		
				30	9	270		
				150		1,230	150	1,350
8				80	9	720	70	630
12				30	9	270	40	360
18	300	10	3,000				340	3,360
22				40	9	360		
				60	10	600		
				100		960	240	2,400
28	20	10	200				260	2,600

(b)

	Receipts			Issues			Balance	
Date	Quantity	Price £	Value £	Quantity	Price £	Value £	Quantity	Value £
October								
1	120	8	960				120	960
3	180	9	1,620				300	2,580
4				150	8.6	1,290	150	1,290
8				80	8.6	688	70	602
12				30	9.0	270	40	332
18	300	10	3,000				340	3,332
22				100	9.8	980	240	2,352
28	20	9.8	196				260	2,548

(c) (i) £1,490

     (ii) £1,438

Jay Ltd Trading Accounts:	*FIFO*	*AVCO*
	£	£
Opening stock	960	960
Purchases (1,620 + 3,000 – 270)	4,350	4,350
	5,310	5,310
Closing stock (parts (a) and (b))	(2,600)	(2,548)
Cost of sales	2,710	2,762
Sales (1,800 + 1,200 + 1,500 – 300)	4,200	4,200
Gross profit	1,490	1,438

(d) (i) The financial statements of most companies are prepared on the **historical** cost convention.

     (ii) In the balance sheet the stocks of the business must be shown at the **lower of cost and net realisable value**.

FINANCIAL STATEMENTS AND RATIO ANALYSIS

17   OWNER OF A BUSINESS

	Sole trader	**Limited company**
Legal entity	The business is not **separate** from the owner.	Companies are **separate legal entities** in law – they can sue and be sued.
Ownership	The business is owned by the **sole trader**.	The company is owned by **shareholders**.
Legal control	Little statutory control.	Companies must comply with company rules being governed by the **Companies Acts**.
Liability	Sole trader has **unlimited liability** to creditors.	The liability of shareholders is **limited to** the capital already introduced by them.
Constitution	No formal constitution required.	The objects, powers and duties of a company must be set out in its **memorandum and articles of association**.
Audit	An audit is not required.	An audit is required (unless **exempt** as a small company) which is a substantial cost.

Management	By the owner.	Separation of management (by **directors**) from ownership (by the **shareholders**).
Returns	The owner takes all the **profit of the business**.	The owners (shareholders) may receive **dividends out of the profits of the business**.
Transfer of ownership	By transfer of the **business itself**.	By transfer of the **shares rather than the business itself**.

18 CASH FLOW STATEMENT

(a) The purpose of a cash flow statement is to provide additional information to the **profit and loss** account and the **balance sheet.** The cash flow statement shows the reasons for the change in the **cash and bank** balances over the accounting period. **Liquidity** is vital to an organisation so the information that the cash flow statement provides is of great use to **users** of the accounts as it is different to the information provided in the **profit and loss account and balance sheet.**

(b) The main use of the cash flow statement is in analysing the **cash movements**. It shows the ability of the organisation to generate cash from **operations** and then shows how that cash has been **spent** over the period. It shows how finance has been serviced in the form of **interest** paid and **equity dividends** paid. It shows monies spent on and received from the sale of **fixed** assets. It also shows receipts and payments for loans and **share capital**.

(c) (i) Current asset investments held as readily disposable stores of value.

(ii) The borrowings of the reporting entity less cash and liquid resources.

(d)

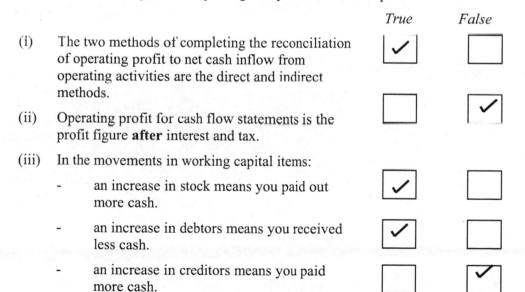

		True	False
(i)	The two methods of completing the reconciliation of operating profit to net cash inflow from operating activities are the direct and indirect methods.	✓	
(ii)	Operating profit for cash flow statements is the profit figure **after** interest and tax.		✓
(iii)	In the movements in working capital items:		
	- an increase in stock means you paid out more cash.	✓	
	- an increase in debtors means you received less cash.	✓	
	- an increase in creditors means you paid more cash.		✓

19 BETA

(a)

	Zeta Ltd	Omega Ltd
Profitability		

Return on capital employed

$$\frac{510}{1,950} \qquad \frac{800}{6,890}$$

$$= 26.2\% \qquad = 11.6\%$$

Return on owners' equity

$$\frac{500}{1,950} \qquad \frac{400}{2,890}$$

$$= 25.6\% \qquad = 13.8\%$$

Gross profit margin

$$\frac{1,000}{4,000} \qquad \frac{1,200}{6,000}$$

$$= 25\% \qquad = 20\%$$

Net operating profit margin

$$\frac{(500+10)}{4,000} \qquad \frac{(400+400)}{6,000}$$

$$= 12.75\% \qquad = 13.3\%$$

Liquidity

Current ratio

$$\frac{1,350}{1,200} \qquad \frac{1,880}{990}$$

$$= 1.13:1 \qquad = 1.90:1$$

Quick ratio

$$\frac{950}{1,200} \qquad \frac{1,080}{990}$$

$$= 0.79:1 \qquad = 1.09:1$$

Working capital management

Stock turnover

$$\frac{400}{3,000} \times 365 \qquad \frac{800}{4,800} \times 365$$

$$= 49 \text{ days} \qquad = 61 \text{ days}$$

Debtor days

$$\frac{800}{4,000} \times 365 \qquad \frac{900}{6,000} \times 365$$

$$= 73 \text{ days} \qquad = 55 \text{ days}$$

Creditor days

$$\frac{800}{3,200} \times 365 \qquad \frac{800}{4,800} \times 365$$

$$= 91 \text{ days} \qquad = 61 \text{ days}$$

(b)

	True	False

(i)   *Profitability*

Zeta has a considerably higher return on capital employed and return on owners' equity than Omega. A contributing factor could be the revaluation of Omega's fixed assets. This would immediately increase capital employed, but would not affect profit. This in turn reduces the return.   ✓ (True)

Zeta has a slightly lower gross profit margin than Omega, which suggests differences in pricing structures.   ✓ (False)

When interest is excluded, Zeta Ltd shows a lower fall in gross profit to operating profit owing to its higher expense figures.   ✓ (False)

(ii)   *Liquidity*

Here Omega shows the better position partly because Zeta has an overdraft and no cash balance.   ✓ (True)

However, Omega has a much lower stock figure. Depending on the reason, this could actually distort the current ratio to give a gloomier picture.   ✓ (False)

(iii)   *Working capital management*

Omega has better credit control for its debtors but it not as successful at turning over stock. Omega may also consider lengthening creditors' payment period to be consistent with the industry average.   ✓ (True)

Zeta has a more efficient stock turnover rate but its debtor and creditor management reinforces its liquidity problem.   ✓ (True)

Both companies are at least paying their creditors after collecting cash from debtors.   ✓ (True)

High gearing suggests a low financial risk.   ✓ (False)

An increase in trade would have more of an impact for Zeta by increasing the margin between the financing interest rate and Zeta's return.   ✓ (False)

20 ARH PLC

(a) *Gross profit ratio*

	20X4	20X5
$\dfrac{\text{Gross profit}}{\text{Sales}} \times 100$	$\dfrac{2,600}{14,400} \times 100$	$\dfrac{4,400}{17,000} \times 100$
	$= 18.1\%$	$= 25.9\%$

Net profit ratio

	20X4	20X5
$\dfrac{\text{Net profit}}{\text{Sales}} \times 100$	$\dfrac{1,400}{14,400} \times 100$	$\dfrac{2,400}{17,000} \times 100$
	$= 9.7\%$	$= 14.1\%$

Return on capital employed

	20X4	20X5
$\dfrac{\text{Net profit}}{\textbf{Average total capital}} \times 100$	$\dfrac{1,400}{6,260} \times 100$	$\dfrac{2,400}{6,210} \times 100$
	$= 22.4\%$	$= 38.6\%$
Average total capital	$\dfrac{(6,700 - 880) + 6,700}{2}$	$\dfrac{6,700 + 5,720}{2}$
	$= 6,260$	$= 6,210$

In 20X5 ARH has managed to increase its turnover by **18%** as well as increasing gross margin and net margin. It is not known whether the increase in turnover is just to do with the increased margins or whether there has been an actual increase in **volume** of sales.

Return on capital employed has also increased and this is due partly to an increased profitability and also partly due to decreased **capital employed**.

	20X4	20X5
Current ratio	**5,700 : 1,500**	**4,420 : 2,700**
	3.8 : 1	**1.6 : 1**
Acid test ratio	**5,700 - 1,300 : 1,500**	**4,420 - 2,000 : 2,700**
	2.9 : 1	**0.9 : 1**

One of the major reasons for the decrease in cash is due to the changes in the **capital** of ARH. The loan of £2.6 million has been paid off over the period and obviously this has had a major impact on the cash balances of the business.

In conclusion, the position of ARH has gone from a very healthy cash position which might even be seen as over cautious to what might be seen as a slightly risky position.

(b) Reserves are profits of a company that have not yet been paid out as dividends.

(c) The revaluation reserve arises when an asset is revalued and the excess over NBV is credited to the revaluation reserve.

Section 5

MOCK ASSESSMENT

(THIS MOCK EXAMINATION IS TO HELP YOU PRACTICE FOR YOUR COMPUTER BASED ASSESSMENT. IT CONTAINS THE SAME NUMBER OF QUESTIONS YOU WILL GET IN A CBA AND SHOULD BE SAT IN 90 MINUTES.)

ALL QUESTIONS ARE COMPULSORY AND MUST BE ATTEMPTED

1   If the owner of a business takes goods from stock for his own personal use, the accounting concept to be considered is the:

    A   prudence concept

    B   capitalisation concept

    C   money measurement concept

    D   separate entity concept.

2   The capital maintenance concept implies that:

    A   the capital of a business should be kept intact by not paying out dividends

    B   a business should invest its profits in the purchase of capital assets

    C   fixed assets should be properly maintained

    D   profit is earned only if the value of an organisation's net assets or its operating capability has increased during the accounting period.

3   A sole trader had net assets of $19,000 at 30 April 20X3. During the year to 30 April 20X3, he introduced $9,800 additional capital into the business. Profits were $8,000, of which he withdrew $4,200. His capital at 1 May 20X2 was:

    A $3,000

    B $5,400

    C $13,000

    D $16,600

4   Which of the following statements concerning a 'true and fair' view is correct?

    A   True and fair has a precise definition which is universally accepted.

    B   There can only be one true and fair view of a company's financial statements.

    C   True and fair means the financial statements are accurate.

    D   True and fair is mainly determined by compliance with generally accepted accounting practice.

5   The draft accounts of Galahad's business for the year ended 31 July 20X0 show a profit of £54,250. However, his accountant notices the following errors:

(i)   Cash drawings of £250 have not been accounted for.

(ii)   Debts amounting to £420, which were provided against in full during the year, should have been written off as bad.

(iii) Rental income of £300 has been classified as interest receivable.

(iv)   On the last day of the accounting period £2,000 in cash was received from a debtor, but no bookkeeping entries have yet been made.

What is the correct profit of the business for the year?

A   £53,580

B   £53,830

C   £54,250

D   £55,830

6   If Sales (including VAT) amounted to £27,612.50, and Purchases (excluding VAT) amounted to £18,000, the balance on the VAT account, assuming all items are subject to VAT at 17.5%, would be:

A   £962.50 debit

B   £962.50 credit

C   £1,682.10 debit

D   £1,682.10 credit

7   You are given the following incomplete and incorrect extract from a trading account of a company that trades at a mark up of 25% on cost:

	£	£
Sales		174,258
Less: Cost of goods sold		
Opening stock	12,274	
Purchases	136,527	
	148,801	
Less: Closing stock	X	
		X
Gross profit		

Having discovered that the sales figure should have been £174,825 and that purchase returns of £1,084 and sales returns of £1,146 have been omitted the closing stock figure should be:

A   £8,662

B   £8,774

C   £17,349

D   £17,458

8   You are given the following figures for sales and debtors, together with certain comparatives:

	20X7	20X6
	£	£
Debtors at year end	74,963	69,472
Sales	697,104	
Total cash received from customers	686,912	
General provision for bad debts	750	695
Specific provision for bad debts	1,264	
Bad debts written off	1,697	

What was the value of sales returns during the year 20X7?

A   £1,740

B   £2,949

C   £3,004

D   £4,268

9   **The capital of a sole trader would change as a result of:**

A   a creditor being paid his account by cheque.

B   raw materials being purchased on credit.

C   fixed assets being purchased on credit.

D   wages being paid in cash.

10   **Your organisation's trial balance at 31 October 20X9 is out of agreement, with the debit side totalling £500 less than the credit side. During November, the following errors are discovered:**

- The sales journal for October had been undercast by £150.

- Rent received of £240 had been credited to the rent payable account.

- The provision for bad debts, which decreased by £420, had been recorded in the provision for bad debts account as an increase.

Following the correction of these errors, the balance on the suspense account would be:

A   Credit £190

B   Credit £670

C   Credit £1,190

D   Debit £1,490

11   **In the quarter ended 31 March 20X2, C Ltd had VAT taxable outputs, net of VAT, of $90,000 and taxable inputs, net of VAT, of $72,000.**

If the rate of VAT is 10%, how much VAT is due?

A $1,800 receivable

B $2,000 receivable

C $1,800 payable

D $2,000 payable

12   **I Ltd operates the imprest system for petty cash. At 1 July there was a float of £150, but it was decided to increase this to £200 from 1 August onwards. During July, the petty cashier received £25 from staff for using the photocopier and a cheque for £90 was cashed for an employee. In July, cheques were drawn for £500 for petty cash.**

How much cash was paid out as cash expenses by the petty cashier in July?

A   £385

B   £435

C   £515

D   £615

13   **What is an audit trail in a computerised accounting system?**

A   A list of all the transactions in a period.

B   A list of all the transactions in a ledger account in a period.

C   A list of all the items checked by the auditor.

D   A list of all the nominal ledger codes.

14 M plc's trial balance did not balance at 31 May 20X1. The following errors were discovered:

Insurance of $500 prepaid at 31 May 20X0 had not been brought down as an opening balance on the insurance amount.

Wages of $5,000 had been incorrectly debited to the purchases account.

The book-keeper had failed to accrue $300 for the telephone invoice owing at 31 May 20X1.

What was the difference on the trial balance?

A $500

B $800

C $5,500

D $5,800

15 At 1 September, the motor expenses account showed 4-months' insurance prepaid of £80 and petrol accrued of £95. During September, the outstanding petrol bill is paid, plus further bills of £245. At 30 September there is a further outstanding petrol bill of £120.

The amount to be shown in the profit and loss account for motor expenses for September is:

A   £385

B   £415

C   £445

D   £460

16 A fixed asset was purchased at the beginning of Year 1 for £2,400 and depreciated by 20% per annum by the reducing balance method. At the beginning of Year 4 it was sold for £1,200. The result of this was:

A   a loss on disposal of £240.00

B   a loss on disposal of £28.80

C   a profit on disposal of £28.80

D   a profit on disposal of £240.00.

17 Stock movements for product X during the last quarter were as follows:

January	Purchases	10 items at £19.80 each
February	Sales	10 items at £30 each
March	Purchases	20 items at £24.50
	Sales	5 items at £30 each

Opening stock at 1 January was 6 items valued at £15 each.

Gross profit for the quarter, using the weighted average cost method, would be:

A   £135.75

B   £155.00

C   £174.00

D   £483.00

18   At 30 September 20X4, Z Ltd had a provision for doubtful debts of £37,000.

During the year ended 30 September 20X5 the company wrote off debts totalling £18,000, and at the end of the year it is decided that the provision for doubtful debts should be £20,000.

What should be included in the profit and loss account for bad and doubtful debts?

A   £35,000 debit

B   £1,000 debit

C   £38,000 debit

D   £1,000 credit

19   Which ONE of the following provides the best explanation of the objective of an internal audit?

A   The objective is to assist directors of a company in the effective discharge of their financial responsibilities towards the members

B   The objective is to provide support to the external auditor

C   The objective is to detect fraud and error

D   The objective is to audit the financial accounts.

20   A fixed asset register had a balance of $125,000. A fixed asset, which had cost $12,000, was sold for $9,000 at a profit of $2,000.

What is the revised balance on the fixed asset register?

A $113,000

B $118,000

C $125,000

D $127,000

21   On 1 May 20X0, A Ltd pays a rent bill of £1,800 for the period to 30 April 20X1. What are the charge to the profit and loss account and the entry in the balance sheet for the year ended 30 November 20X0?

A   £1,050 charge to profit and loss account and prepayment of £750 in the balance sheet.

B   £1,050 charge to profit and loss account and accrual of £750 in the balance sheet.

C   £1,800 charge to profit and loss account and no entry in the balance sheet.

D   £750 charge to profit and loss account and prepayment of £1,050 in the balance sheet.

22   W bought a new printing machine from abroad. The cost of the machine was £80,000. The installation costs were £5,000 and the employees received specific training on how to use this particular machine, at a cost of £2,000. Before using the machine to print customers' orders, a test was undertaken and the paper and ink cost £1,000.

What should be the cost of the machine in the company's balance sheet?

A   £80,000

B   £85,000

C   £87,000

D   £88,000

23   Your firm values stock using the weighted average cost method. At 1 October 20X8, there were 60 units in stock valued at £12 each. On 8 October, 40 units were purchased for £15 each, and a further 50 units were purchased for £18 each on 14 October. On 21 October, 75 units were sold for £1,200.

The value of closing stock at 31 October 20X8 was:

A   £900

B   £1,020

C   £1,110

D   £1,125

24   A fixed asset was disposed of for £2,200 during the last accounting year. It had been purchased exactly three years earlier for £5,000, with an expected residual value of £500, and had been depreciated on the reducing balance basis, at 20% per annum.

The profit or loss on disposal was:

A   £360 loss

B   £150 loss

C   £104 loss

D   £200 profit

25   At 1 January 20X3 the capital structure of Q Limited was as follows:

	£
Issued share capital 1,000,000 ordinary shares of 50p each	500,000
Share premium account	300,000

On 1 April 20X3 the company made an issue of 200,000 50p shares at £1.30 each, and on 1 July the company made a bonus (capitalisation) issue of one share for every four in issue at the time, using the share premium account for the purpose.

Which of the following correctly states the company's share capital and share premium account at 31 December 20X3?

	Share capital	Share premium account
A	£750,000	£230,000
B	£875,000	£285,000
C	£750,000	£310,000
D	£750,000	£610,000

26   The following is an extract from the balance sheets of FRC plc for the years ended 31 July 20X1 and 31 July 20X2:

	20X3 £000	20X2 £000
Stock	50	80
Debtors	60	50
Creditors	35	30
Accruals	5	20

What figure would appear in the cash flow statement of FRC plc for the year ended 31 July 20X3 as part of the cash flow from operations?

A   £25,000 outflow

B   £10,000 outflow

C   £10,000 inflow

D   £25,000 inflow

27   Your company's profit and loss account for the year ended 30 September 20X8 showed the following:

	£000
Net profit before interest and tax	1,200
Interest	200
	1,000
Corporation tax	400
Retained profit for the year	600

Its balance sheet at 30 September 20X7 showed the following capital:

	£000
Share capital	8,000
Profit and loss account balance	1,200
	9,200
10% debenture	2,000
	11,200

Return on average capital employed for the year ended 30 September 20X8 is:

A   5.88%

B   10.17%

C   10.43%

D   none of these.

28   A business commenced with a bank balance of £3,250; it subsequently purchased goods on credit for £10,000; gross profit mark-up was 120%; half the goods were sold for cash, less cash discount of 5%; all takings were banked.

The resulting net profit was:

A   £700

B   £3,700

C   £5,450

D   £5,700

29   Which of the following would cause a company's net profit to increase?

A   Issue of 100,000 ordinary shares at a premium of 2%

B   Revaluation of a freehold property from £70,000 to £100,000

C   Disposal of a fork lift truck which originally cost £15,000 and has a net book value of £9,250 for £8,500

D   Receipt of £25 from a debtor previously written off as bad

30   Which of the following is not a permitted use of the share premium account?

A   Financing the issue of partly-paid bonus shares

B   Writing off preliminary expenses on the formation of a company

C   Providing the premium payable on the redemption of debentures

D   Writing off expenses of share issues

31   You are given the following information for the year ended 31 October 20X7:

	£
Purchases of raw materials	112,000
Returns inwards	8,000
Decrease in stocks of raw materials	8,000
Direct wages	42,000
Carriage outwards	4,000
Carriage inwards	3,000
Production overheads	27,000
Increase in work-in-progress	10,000

The value of factory cost of goods completed is:

A   £174,000

B   £182,000

C   £183,000

D   £202,000

32   During September, your organisation had sales of £148,000, which made a gross profit of £40,000. Purchases amounted to £100,000 and opening stock was £34,000.

The value of closing stock was:

A   £24,000

B   £26,000

C   £42,000

D   £54,000

33   A business's bank balance increased by £750,000 during its last financial year. During the same period it issued shares of £1 million and repaid a debenture of £750,000. It purchased fixed assets for £200,000 and charged depreciation of £100,000. Working capital (other than the bank balance) increased by £575,000.

Its profit for the year was:

A   £1,175,000

B   £1,275,000

C   £1,325,000

D   £1,375,000

34   A company's gearing ratio would rise if:

A   a decrease in long-term loans is LESS than a decrease in shareholders' funds

B   a decrease in long-term loans is MORE than a decrease in shareholders' funds

C   interest rates rose

D   dividends were paid.

35   The gross profit mark-up is 40% where:

A   sales are £120,000 and gross profit is £48,000

B   sales are £120,000 and cost of sales is £72,000

C   sales are £100,800 and cost of sales is £72,000

D   sales are £100,800 and cost of sales is £60,480.

36   Revenue reserves would decrease if a company:

A   sets aside profits to pay future dividends

B   transfers amounts into 'general reserves'

C   issues shares at a premium

D   pays dividends.

37   The following information relates to a business at its year end:

	£000
Sales	600
Stocks at beginning of year:	
Raw materials	20
Work-in-progress	4
Finished goods	68
Stocks at end of year:	
Raw materials	22
Work-in-progress	8
Finished goods	60
Purchases of raw materials	100
Returns inwards	10
Returns outwards	15
Carriage inwards	8
Carriage outwards	12
Direct labour	80

The prime cost of goods manufactured during the year is:

A   £111,000

B   £163,000

C   £171,000

D   £176,000

38   A business has the following capital and long-term liabilities.

	31.10.X8	31.10.X9
	£ million	£ million
12% Debentures	20	40
Issued share capital	15	30
Share premium	3	18
Retained profits	22	12

At 31 October 20X9, its gearing ratio, compared to that at 31 October 20X8, has:

A   risen, resulting in greater risk for shareholders.

B   risen, resulting in greater security for shareholders.

C   fallen, resulting in greater security for shareholders.

D   remained the same.

39   A company had the following gross profit calculation in its last accounting period:

	£
Sales	130,000
Cost of sales	60,000
Gross profit	70,000

Average stock during that period was £7,500.

In the next accounting period, sales are expected to increase by 40% and the rate of stock turnover is expected to double. If average stock remains at £7,500 the gross profit mark-up percentage will be:

A   30.0%

B   34.1%

C   51.7%

D   65.9%

40   In 20X1, a company's current ratio was 2.5 : 1 and its acid test ratio was 0.8 : 1. By the end of 20X2, the ratios are expected to be 3 : 1 and 0.6 : 1 respectively. These changes are most likely to be due to which ONE of the following?

A   Increased bank balances

B   Decreased bank balances

C   Increased stocks

D   Increased debtors and creditors

Section 6

ANSWERS TO MOCK ASSESSMENT

1 D

The separate entity concept is that the affairs of the owner are separate from those of the business. The business and its owner should be regarded as separate from each other, with the business 'owing' its capital to the owner. Consequently, if the owner of a business uses goods taken from the stock of the business for personal use, they have been withdrawn from the business and will be recorded as drawings, i.e. a withdrawal of capital.

2 D

Answer D gives a good summary of the capital maintenance concept. Profit cannot be earned unless the capital of the business has been maintained (ignoring any new capital introduced during the period and ignoring dividends/drawings). In historical cost accounting, capital is maintained if the net assets of the business are the same at the end of the period as at the beginning of the period.

3 B

	$	$
Capital at 30 April 20X3		19,000
Capital introduced in the year		(9,800)
Profit for the year	(8,000)	
Drawings	4,200	
Retained profit		(3,800)
Capital at 1 May 20X2		5,400

4 D

True and fair is a difficult concept to define in a single phrase or sentence. It is mainly determined by compliance with generally accepted accounting practice. The incorrect definitions in the question imply that 'true and fair' has a precise meaning or interpretation.

5 C

None of the errors affects the amount of profit.

6 B

VAT account				
	£			£
VAT on purchases (input tax) (18,000 × 17.5%)	3,150.0	VAT on sales (output tax) (27,612.5 × (17.5/117.5))		4,112.5
Balance carried forward	962.5			
	4,112.5			4,112.5

7   B

	£	£	£	
Sales			174,825	
Less: Sales returns			1,146	
			173,679	*(125%)*
Less: Cost of goods sold				
Opening stock		12,274		
Purchases	136,527			
Less: Purchase returns	1,084			
		135,443		
		147,717		
Less: Closing stock		(8,774)		
Cost of sales			138,943	*(100%)*
Gross profit			34,736	*(25%)*

8   C

Debtors ledger control account

	£		£
Balance b/f	69,472	Cash received	686,912
Sales	697,104	Write-offs	1,697
		Returns	3,004
		Balance c/f	74,963
	766,576		766,576

9   D

For a sole trader, capital = net assets.

If a creditor is paid by cheque, both creditors and cash are reduced, but net assets remain the same.

If raw materials are purchased on credit, both stock and creditors are increased, but net assets remain the same.

If fixed assets are purchased on credit, both fixed assets and creditors are increased, but net assets remain the same.

If wages are paid in cash, cash reduces and therefore net assets have fallen.

10   A

Suspense account

	£		£
Balance transferred in from trial balance	500	Decrease in provision for bad debts recorded as an increase	840
Sales journal undercast	150		
Balance c/d	190		
	840		840

11   C

Output VAT is VAT on sales and input VAT is tax on purchases and other expenses.

	$
Outputs, net of VAT	90,000
Inputs, net of VAT	72,000
Excess of outputs over inputs	18,000
VAT payable at 10%	$1,800

12   A

Petty cash account

	£		£
Opening balance	150	Cheque cashed	90
Photocopying	25	Payments (bal fig)	385
Bank	500	Closing balance	200
	675		675

13   A

An audit trail is a list of all the transactions in a period.

14   A

Insurance balance omitted:	$500
Wages misposted – does not affect trial balance:	nil
Accrual omitted – does not affect trial balance:	nil

15   A

	£
Expenses paid in the month	245
Unpaid petrol expense	120
Insurance (1/4 of prepayment brought forward)	20
Motor expenses for September	385

Note: The payment of the accrued expense from August does not affect the September expenses.

16   B

		£
Year 1	Cost	2,400.0
	Depreciation	(480.0)
Year 2	Net book value	1,920.0
	Depreciation	(384.0)
Year 3	Net book value	1,536.0
	Depreciation	(307.2)
Year 4	Net book value	1,228.8
	Sale value	1,200.0
	Loss on disposal	(28.8)

17   B

	Items	Unit value	
		£	£
Opening stock	6	15	90
January: purchases	10	19.80	198
	16	18	288
February: sales	(10)	18	(180)
	6	18	108
March: purchases	20	24.50	490
	26	23	598
March: sales	(5)	23	(115)
	21	23	483

	£
Sales (15 x £30)	450
Cost of sales (£180 = £115)	(295)
Gross profit	155

18   B

	£
Bad debts written off	18,000
Reduction in provision for doubtful debts	(17,000)
Net charge for bad and doubtful debts	1,000

A charge is an expense, which is a debit balance item.

19   A

The objective of an internal audit is to assist directors of a company in the effective discharge of their financial responsibilities towards the members.

20   B

	$	$
Original balance on fixed asset register		125,000
Net book value of assets sold:		
Proceeds	9,000	
Less: Profit	(2,000)	
		(7,000)
Adjusted balance		118,000

21   A

P&L charge £1,800 × 7/12 = £1,050

Prepayment £1,800 × 5/12 = £750

22   D

A tangible fixed asset should be measured initially at its cost. 'Cost' means the directly attributable costs of bringing the asset into working condition for its intended use. These include the purchase cost, initial delivery and handling costs, installation costs (including the cost of 'own employees' labour if they are involved in the construction/installation of the asset) and professional fees. Capitalisation of directly attributable costs should cease when the asset is ready for use, even if it has not actually been brought into use. The costs of commissioning and start-up are only included in cost where the asset would be incapable of operating at normal levels without the commissioning or start-up period.

On this basis, it is not clear whether training and testing costs can be included in the fixed asset cost. CIMA's official answer was that they could be included.

	£
Purchase cost of machine	80,000
Installation	5,000
Training	2,000
Testing	1,000
Fixed asset cost	88,000

23   C

Date		Units	Unit value £	Stock value £
1 October	Opening stock	60		720
8 October	Purchase 40 units at £15	40		600
14 October	Purchase 50 units at £18	50		900
		150	14.80	2,220
21 October	Sold 75 units: cost	(75)	14.80	(1,110)
31 October	Closing stock	75	14.80	1,110

24   A

	£
Cost	5,000
Year 1 (20% × 5,000)	(1,000)
Year 2 (20% × 4,000)	(800)
Year 3 (20% × 3,200)	(640)
Net book value at time of disposal	2,560
Sale proceeds	2,200
Loss on disposal	360

25   C

The addition to share premium with the rights issue is 200,000 shares at (£1.30 - £0.50) each, i.e. £160,000.

	Share capital £000	Share premium £000
At start of period	500	300
Rights issue	100	160
	600	460
Bonus issue	150	(150)
At end of period	750	310

26   C

	£000
Change in working capital	
Decrease in stock	30
Increase in debtors	(10)
Decrease in creditors (30 + 20) – (35 + 5)	(10)
Net cash inflow	10

27   C

Capital employed at the start of the year (in £000) = 11,200

Capital employed at the end of the year (in £000) = 11,200 + retained profit 600 = 11,800.

Average capital employed (in £000) = (11,200 + 11,800)/2 = 11,500.

Return = profit before interest and taxation = (in £000) 1,200.

Return on average capital employed = (1,200/11,500) × 100% = 10.43%

28   C

Cost of goods sold = £5,000.

Profit mark-up = 120% = £6,000.

Sale price = £5,000 + £6,000 = £11,000.

Discounts allowed = 5% of £11,000 = £550.

	£
Gross profit	6,000
Discounts allowed	550
Net profit	5,450

29   D

The premium on the issue of shares must be put into the Share Premium Account. The surplus on revaluation of the property must be put into the Revaluation Reserve. The disposal of the truck results in a loss. The payment by a debtor whose debt has already been written off as bad will increase profit. (The bad debts expense will be reduced, so profit will increase.)

30   A

The share premium account can be used to finance the issue of fully-paid bonus shares, but not partly-paid bonus shares.

31   B

	£
Purchase of raw materials	112,000
Decrease in stocks of raw materials	8,000
Direct wages	42,000
Carriage inwards	3,000
Production overheads	27,000
Increase in work in progress	(10,000)
Value of factory cost of goods completed	182,000

32   B

	£	£
Sales		148,000
Opening stock	34,000	
Purchases (20,000 – 4,000)	100,000	
	134,000	
Closing stock (balancing figure)	(26,000)	
Cost of sales (148,000 – 40,000)		108,000
Gross profit		40,000

33   A

	£000
Profit for the year	1,175
Add back depreciation	100
Less: Increase in working capital	(575)
Cash flow from operating activities	700
Add: Cash from issue of shares	1,000

Less: Repayment of debentures	(750)	
Less: Purchase of fixed assets	(200)	
Increase in bank balance	750	

34   D

The payment of a dividend reduces equity and so gearing will rise. Answer A might also be correct, but only if the company has a gearing ratio of 100% or more. If gearing is less than 100%, answer A would not necessarily be correct. (For example, if total long-term debt is 100 and equity is 200, the gearing ratio is 50%. If debt now falls by 20 and equity by 30, the new gearing ratio would be lower at (80/170) 47%.

35   C

You might need to answer this by testing each answer in turn.

$$\frac{\text{Gross profit}}{\text{Cost of sales}} \quad \frac{28,800}{72,000} = 40\%$$

	£
Sales	100,800
Cost of sales	(72,000)
Gross profit	28,800

36   D

Revenue reserves are reserves out of which dividends can be paid. Answers A and B would have no effect on revenue reserves. (General reserve is a part of revenue reserves.) Answer C also has no effect on revenue reserves, since it involves the issue of capital, and the share premium account would increase. A payment of dividend reduces the profit and loss reserve, which is a revenue reserve.

37   C

	£000	£000
Direct materials:		
Opening stock of raw materials	20	
Purchases (100 – 15)	85	
Carriage inwards	8	
	113	
Closing stock of raw materials	(22)	
Raw materials in cost of production		91
Direct labour		80
Prime cost of manufacturing in the period		171

Note: You might have thought that the question was asking for the prime cost of finished output in the period, in which case you would need to make an adjustment for the net increase in working capital in the period by £4,000. The prime cost of goods output to finished goods in the periods was £171,000 - £4,000 -= £167,000, which is not an available answer. However, prime cost is usually taken to mean the prime cost of manufacturing in the period.

38   A

$$\text{Gearing 31 October X8} = \frac{20}{15+3+22+20} = 33.3\%$$

$$\text{Gearing 31 October X9} = \frac{40}{30+18+12+40} = 40\%$$

Gearing is a measure of risk: increased gearing indicates increased risk.

39 B

Current stock turnover = (7,500/60,000) × 12 months = 1.5 months.

If the rate of stock turnover double, stock turnover will halve to 0.75 months.

If average stock is £7,500, the cost of sales will be:

£7,500 × (12/0.75) = £120,000.

	£
Sales (130,000 x 1.4)	182,000
Cost of sales	120,000
Gross profit	62,000
Gross profit as % of sales	34.1%

40 C

The current ratio (ratio of current assets to current liabilities) is expected to rise but the acid test ratio (ratio of current assets excluding stocks to current liabilities) is expected to fall. This would occur if stock levels went up by a large amount, whilst the balances for debtors and cash fell.